Armin Kriechbaumer

Yorkshire Terriers

Second Edition

Everything about Purchase, Care, Nutrition, Breeding, Behavior, and Training

With 26 color photos
by Sally Anne Thompson

Drawings by György Jankovics

Translated from the German by
Kathleen Luft

Consulting Editor:
Matthew M. Vriends, Ph.D.

BARRON'S

Contents

This Yorkie is keeping a close eye on the little toy mouse.

Preface

Without a doubt, the Yorkshire terrier is one of the most attractive small dogs. Affectionate, lovable, but independent, high-spirited, and alert as well—that characterizes the Yorkie to a T. To help your Yorkshire terrier develop these positive qualities, and to keep its strong will from turning into obstinacy, you need to train it lovingly and consistently and provide it with the proper living conditions.

In this Barron's pet owner's manual you'll find all you need to know about the origin of the Yorkshire terrier and the characteristics of the breed. Based on his experience, the author provides helpful suggestions that tell you what to look for when you buy a Yorkie and how to make your puppy's adjustment to your household easier. He presents easy-to-follow instructions for grooming the Yorkie's coat, providing proper nutrition, and keeping your pet healthy. The book includes valuable information for anyone interested in breeding or showing a Yorkshire terrier.

The HOW-TO pages deal with basic training, good ways to spend time with your pet, coat care, and first aid procedures in the event of illness or injury.

Informative drawings by György Jankovics bring the text to life. Beautiful color photos, taken by Sally Anne Thompson, provide a glimpse of this little dog's intriguing personality, which has made the breed so popular throughout the world.

The author and the editors of Barron's series of pet owners' books wish you a great deal of pleasure with your Yorkshire terrier.

Please read the "Important Note" on page 63.

Basic Facts about Yorkshire Terriers

Sassy Yet So Lovable

The Yorkshire terrier has not always possessed the great popularity it enjoys today. Even in the early 1980s people out for a walk would stop and inquire about the glossy-coated creature at the end of the leash. The dog's physical appearance—its diminutive size, its long, silky hair, and the roguish look in its eye—attracted everyone's attention. The red bow often found in the golden hair on its head was eye-catching, too. The explanation that this was the tiniest member of the large terrier family was greeted with amazement. Meanwhile, the Yorkshire terrier has become one of the most beloved small dog breeds.

High-spirited and tireless: A well-groomed Yorkie is a sight to make hearts leap with joy. A cheerful, affectionate member of the family, this dog is always in the mood for fun, and its innate high spirits continually keep its owner on the go. Anyone who describes the Yorkie as a lap dog does not really know this bundle of energy. Playing, racing around, digging in holes in the ground, sniffing—these are all activities the Yorkshire terrier loves, along with exploring its surroundings on lengthy walks and hikes. Despite its small size, it is a tireless runner; if it keeps in training, it easily can run 6 to 9 miles (10–15 km) at a time.

An alert, good family dog: From its terrier ancestors, the Yorkie inherited the qualities that make it an ideal watchdog, including a generous helping of hunting instinct. It will fearlessly defend its own property and that of its owner. Most of all, it enjoys being near "its family" at all times, and it eagerly accompanies family members wherever they go. Its diminutive size and friendly nature make the Yorkie easy to take along almost everywhere. A curious dog, it wants to know everything that is going on around it, which also explains why the Yorkie adapts so quickly to new surroundings and can adjust to different conditions. The Yorkie is easy to keep, even in a fairly small apartment—provided it gets a daily outing, of course—though it also appreciates a house with a yard. Another thing that makes the Yorkie such a good indoor pet is the fact that unlike other breeds, it does not shed twice a year, despite its luxuriant coat. Daily grooming with a comb and brush is all that is necessary.

Independent and of strong character: The Yorkie could almost be called the cat of the dog world. On velvety paws it explores its domain and "creeps" into the hearts of all the family members, who, if they aren't careful, will be trained by the Yorkie, and not the other way around. Usually it will achieve what it sets out to do, through self-assurance and innate diplomacy. The Yorkie is adaptable, equipped with a good deal of stubbornness, proud,

Everything interests a puppy. This little Yorkie even makes itself comfortable in a shoe.

Despite its small stature, the Yorkie has remained a true terrier. This frisky, high-spirited, independent dog has a great longing for activity. If you think of your pet merely as a lap dog, its life will be boring and tedious.

The Yorkie keeps a watchful eye on everything going on around it.

intelligent, lovable, full of energy, and, despite its small size, a dog to be treated with respect, in no way inferior to the larger members of the species in spirit, courage, and perseverance.

Origin of the Breed

The Yorkshire terrier originated in England. Quite early the inhabitants of that island developed a special relationship to dogs, along with a strong drive to breed them. We assume that the roots of the Yorkshire terrier, and many other terrier breeds as well, are to be found in the Highlands of Scotland. The history of the breed's origin, however, can be traced back with relative accuracy only as far as the middle of the eighteenth century.

The Ancestors of the Yorkshire Terrier

In preindustrial England, the serfs of the ruling class were allowed to keep only dogs under a certain size that, it was thought, would be unfit for hunting. Since all the game was reserved exclusively for the aristocracy, this rule was meant to keep the poor from training their dogs to poach. Gamekeepers checked the size of the dogs with a kind of loop, about 7 inches (18 cm) in diameter, through which the dogs had to squeeze. If the dog made it through the loop, its master was allowed to keep it.

The serfs were anxious to breed small but robust dogs that conformed with the requirements of the law but could be used in hunting as well. Since the poor themselves had barely enough to eat, these dogs could expect no food from their owners. To feed themselves, therefore, they pursued primarily rats and mice and occasionally provided their master with small game that they had attacked and torn to pieces.

The waterside terrier: In the eighteenth and nineteenth centuries, dogs with long, smooth coats having a bluish sheen were common in the county of Yorkshire, in northern England. They roamed the countryside, preferring to stay near rivers and canals, the major trade routes of the day. There they lived largely on the garbage they found along the banks. The people who hauled goods on their boats soon began to take these friendly dogs on board as companions, and there they made themselves useful as "sanitary police," hunting uninvited rodents.

This dog, which was given the name "waterside terrier," today is considered one of the earliest ancestors of the Yorkie.

The Clydesdale and Paisley terriers: With the beginning of industrialization in England toward the end of the eighteenth century, many workers came from Scotland, which was even poorer than England, to find employment in the weaving mills of Yorkshire. Many Scots brought along their dogs, which at the time were collectively known as "Scotch terriers." In reality, however, they belonged to several breeds that only later were assigned more accurate names. Among them were the Clydesdale and Paisley terriers, both of which had long, silky, bluish coats and semierect ears. Both breeds have since become extinct. It is thought today that the Clydesdale terrier had a decisive influence on the physical appearance of the Yorkshire terrier.

Not until the beginning of the nineteenth century were efforts made to catalog the dogs that were systematically bred. For the working class, breeding dogs was more than a hobby. It represented a welcome source of extra income, however minuscule. For that reason the details of the various experimental crossings were kept secret and that is why so little is known about them today.

Huddersfield Ben, for example, was the product of a carefully planned breeding. Born in 1865, he is considered the forefather of all Yorkshire terriers. His appearance at dog shows earned him the nickname "prince of dogs." He called forth enormous attention and admiration and won more than 70 prizes. He was extremely successful in the rat-killing contests popular at that time. Although he died when only six years old, he had so many descendants that from then on a new breed was developed: the Yorkshire terrier.

Yorkshire Terriers in America

We are no better informed about the introduction of the Yorkshire terrier into America and its development here than we are about its earlier history in England. We know, however, that Yorkies have been in America since 1880 and that the breed has steadily gained in popularity. The American fanciers are most interested in very small Yorkshire terriers, and frequently give great importance to coat quality. Though American breeders are, in general, not as fussy

about the total number of teeth as are most of the European breeders, they do appreciate a "good bite," meaning level and properly set teeth.

Meet the Yorkshire Terrier

The first standard: In 1886 this breed was first entered in the register of the English Kennel Club, the parent organization that oversees the English breed clubs. An official standard was put together in 1896. In contrast to other small dog breeds of that day, which were crossed with a great variety of breeds to give them a cuter, more doll-like appearance, the Yorkshire terrier was selectively reproduced through linebreeding (a form of inbreeding that involves the mating of members of the same family, such as the grandmother by the son, usually in hope of perpetuating a particular feature). Only the best of the offspring were used in subsequent breeding programs.

Breeders in those days had a sure sense. They deserve the credit for having preserved the most typical features of the Yorkie, which at the same time ran counter to the swiftly changing trends of fashion.

The early ancestor of the Yorkshire terrier: Huddersfield Ben (left), his daughter Katie (right).

Romping in the yard is twice as much fun with a companion, whether the activity is sniffing, digging in the ground, or engaging in a contest of strength. And when there is something else to inspect—as shown here, the overturned flowerpot—the inquisitive Yorkies are always on hand.

The Yorkie today: The Yorkie's physical appearance, so familiar to us today, was well established by the turn of the century. Beginning in the 1960s, the breed became increasingly well known, and quite soon the Yorkie—unfortunately—became a "fashionable dog." Unscrupulous "dog propagaters" took advantage of that fact, to the detriment of the breed. To counteract this negative trend, breed fanciers founded special Yorkie clubs devoted to responsible breeding.

The Yorkie has remained a true terrier and a dog that is in no way inferior; despite its small stature, it possesses all the attributes that an anatomically well-developed dog exhibits. City dwellers, in particular, found in the Yorkshire terrier a cheerful dog that could adapt to urban living conditions. Today the Yorkie is one of the best-loved small dog breeds in the world.

The Breed Standard

The standard describes in detail the ideal type of a particular breed; it covers both the dog's physical appearance and its character traits. The breed standard is issued in the country of origin of the breed in question. In the Yorkshire terrier's case, it was issued in England in 1896. It is recorded with the international parent organization that oversees all dog breeders and is passed on to the respective member clubs, so that uniform criteria for judging each breed are available. All the specifications are mandatory, and they are always laid down in a studbook. They are considered to be the basis for all breeding programs, as well as for judging a purebred dog at breed shows and other dog shows. Breeders, dog clubs, and show judges have to adhere to the guidelines of the breed standard.

If you intend to breed or show your Yorkie, you should buy one that conforms as closely as possible to the ideal type described in the breed standard. However, if you have no such ambitions, you'll be just as happy with a Yorkie that is healthy and of excellent character, though its physical appearance may deviate slightly from the standard.

Distribution of colors in a Yorkie, as prescribed by the breed standard. Light areas: golden tan. Dark areas: steel blue.

Guidelines of the Standard

The most important parts of the breed standard for the Yorkshire terrier prescribe the following features and traits:

General appearance: A lively and intelligent toy terrier, courageous and with an even disposition. Its long, straight hair is parted on the nose and all the way down the back to the tip of the tail. The overall shape should be compact and well-proportioned, and the erect posture should command admiration.

Head: Small, flat, and not too rounded. The muzzle should not be too long. The nose should be black. The eyes should be medium large, dark, bright, and with an alert, intelligent expression. The teeth should meet in a

Yorkie Profile

Breed: Yorkshire terrier.
Group: Terriers.
Country of origin: England.
Weight: Ideal weight between 4 and 6 pounds (1.8–2.8 kg).
Character: Lively, fearless, and alert, but lovable, affectionate, and very playful as well.
Suitable for: People who want to keep a small, but "real" dog (possibly in a small city apartment) and can find enough time to groom its coat.
Not suitable for: People who shy away from time-consuming coat care or who want to keep the Yorkie as a lap dog.
Requirements: Despite its small size, the Yorkie has to be taken out every day, and owners must spend a great deal of time with their pet. The Yorkie does not like being alone.

perfect, regular scissor bite, though a level bite is acceptable. The small, V-shaped ears should stand upright and not be set too far apart. Their proportions should be in keeping with the head. Drop ears and hanging ears are not permitted.

Body: Compact; short, but not square in shape; straight back line and powerful flanks.

Feet: Rounded, with black claws.

Tail: Docked to a medium length, with plenty of hair; carried slightly higher than the level of the back (but not stiffly).

Coat: This is the most important characteristic of the breed. The body hair should be moderately long, absolutely smooth (not wavy), and fine and silky in texture.

Color: From the back of the head down to the tip of the tail, the Yorkie should be steel blue, with no admixture of pale, brown, or black hairs. On the head and chest, the hair should be a rich tan (yellow gold, not red gold). It should be darker at the roots than at the midportion of the hair shaft, becoming somewhat lighter at the tip. The shaded tan should never reach higher than the elbow or the stifle (see drawing, page 10).

Weight: Must not exceed 7 pounds (3.2 kg); the ideal weight lies between 4 and 6 pounds (1.8–2.8 kg).

Faulty posture: Roach back, sloping rump, tail carried too high.

Faulty posture: Too deep in the shoulders, hindquarters too high.

Suggestions for Would-be Buyers

Will a Yorkie Suit Your Lifestyle?

You need to give careful consideration to this question long before you set out to buy a Yorkie. Take plenty of time for your deliberations, and never buy a dog on a momentary whim! Your new friend will be spending the next 10 or 15 years with you, and that means that you are taking on a major—and, above all, long-term—responsibility. In certain respects you will have to totally change your thus far "dog-free" life. Find out all you can about the character and special features of your future housemate, to avoid surprises later.

Basic Considerations

• Will the landlord allow you to keep a dog? Check the terms of your lease.
• Are your living conditions appropriate for the needs of a Yorkie? Even though the dog can easily be kept in a small apartment, it still needs daily outings.
• Do you have enough time for the Yorkie? Dogs are pack animals, and for their mental development they need close contact with humans. Your Yorkie should not spend the entire day alone. At least once a day you have to take your pet for a fairly long walk and give it a great deal of attention at other times as well. Even in bad weather, it needs to be taken out to relieve itself several times a day.

• Do you have time to consistently train your pet? Even a small dog like the Yorkie has to be taught the basics, unless you want to degrade it into the role of lap dog.
• Are you willing to bear the costs of necessary preventive care and treatment by a veterinarian if your Yorkie gets sick?
• Who can be counted on to take care of your dog if you have to go to a hospital or retirement home, or on a business trip, or you cannot take your pet along on vacation?
• Are all the family members in agreement about the acquisition of a dog?
• Is any member of your family allergic to dog hair? If you are unsure, consult your physician before buying a dog.

Male or Female?

In my own dogs, I have never observed any substantial gender-related differences in temperament or character, but consider the following:.

Neighborhood conditions: Look around to see whether your neighbors' dogs are male or female. If the majority are females, your male would try with all his might to get to any female dog once she comes into heat. Restlessness and perpetual marking would be the result. If predominantly male dogs live in your area, you have to expect "gentlemen callers" on a frequent basis while your female dog is in heat.

A puppy likes to chew on everything. If you don't want that to include your own shoe, give your pet a rawhide substitute—it is healthy and an ideal toy.

Young Yorkies love to play. With two dogs, games are even more fun.

Differences in keeping: Female dogs come into heat twice a year. The bleeding can last up to 15 days, but it usually is not very pronounced in small dogs like the Yorkie. To keep your furnishings from becoming soiled, you can have your bitch wear special protective panties (available in pet stores). When male dogs mark, the long hair hanging down their sides gets dirty, and these areas need to be cleaned with a damp cloth after every walk.

Puppy or Full-grown Dog?

A puppy: I generally advise people to buy a puppy because teaching a young dog is such a rewarding experience. It is exciting to watch the various stages of development. At such an early age, the little Yorkie has a chance to grow into the family and become imprinted by it, so that a close bond is formed.

A full-grown dog: If you are looking for an older dog that is already trained, you should make inquiries at breeders. In kennels with quite a few dogs, the breeding stock sometimes gets superannuated. That is why breeders have started occasionally to give up five- or six-year-old dogs to dog lovers. Even though these animals have been kept under excellent conditions, they have had to share their keeper's attentions with a number of other dogs, which makes it easier for them to adjust to a new home than for other full-grown dogs.

Occasionally a Yorkie will become available because illness or relocation forces its owner to give it up. Although such a change is always a major upheaval in a dog's life, a Yorkshire terrier, with its independent character, has a somewhat easier time adjusting to a new family than other breeds do, but be aware that occasionally, a Yorkshire terrier that has had to change owners "forgets" its house training and other schooling for a short time.

One Yorkie or Two?

A Yorkie does not necessarily have to have another member of its species under the same roof in order to be happy. If you acquire a second Yorkie, however, your burden will be somewhat relieved, since the two dogs will interact with one another. Space is not a problem, but your expenditures for upkeep and veterinary care will double.

If you decide to get a second Yorkie, don't wait too long after buying your first one since the "occupant" of the

territory will engage in acts of defiance and petty rivalries. If you already own a full-grown dog, it is best to buy a puppy, which the older dog generally will accept without difficulty. Make sure that the first dog retains all its old rights, and never neglect it in favor of the new arrival.

My tip: Buy two dogs of the same sex at one time. That will prevent problems during the bitch's estrous cycle.

Yorkies and Other Pets

As a rule, a Yorkie doesn't have a hard time accepting other pets. Keep in mind, however, that its nature will always be that of a terrier; eager for knowledge, your pet will sniff curiously at everything that is unfamiliar.

With small pets such as hamsters, guinea pigs, and birds, never leave the dog with the other animal unsupervised. It might regard the smaller pet as prey and chase it.

Cats will be accepted by the Yorkie if they live in the same household; however, the dog is more likely to chase strange cats.

With other dog breeds the Yorkie generally can establish a good relationship, since it usually is smart enough to recognize the superiority of a bigger dog. If it feels cornered, however, it will defend itself energetically. That can lead to fights involving biting, with resulting injuries.

Yorkies and Children

The Yorkie's lovable nature and love of play make it an ideal partner for a child. The close contact with the animal molds the child and promotes his or her development. In addition, the child

The mother dog keeps a close watch on her two puppies.

acquires a sense of duty and learns to show consideration of others.

Smaller children should always be supervised when playing with the Yorkie, since clumsy young fingers can sometimes inadvertently cause a little dog great pain.

Older children can be made to understand that the Yorkie may be a playmate, but it is never a plaything, and it needs to be treated accordingly. The dog is a living being in its own right, and its needs and peculiarities have to be respected.

Dos and Don'ts for Yorkie Buyers

The enormous popularity of the Yorkshire terrier caused the demand for this friendly small dog to grow by leaps and bounds. That, in turn, led a number of unscrupulous animal dealers to produce puppies in large numbers, without regard for the dogs' health or the requirements of the breed standard. Only reputable breeders can guarantee that you are receiving a healthy dog with no anatomical faults and with the traits of character typical of the breed.

Where to Buy a Yorkshire Terrier

Your safest bet is to ask someone at the local Yorkshire terrier clubs (see Useful Literature and Addresses, page 62) where you can obtain a puppy. The dealers and breeders whose names you will be given are certain to be reputable and reliable. The breed associations keep track of the puppies by registering them in the studbook. Buying from a knowledgeable dealer or breeder also gives you a chance to pick out your own puppy and to get sound advice. The puppies are already vaccinated and wormed, and you receive a pedigree, a

vaccination record, and a feeding plan for the first few weeks.

Where Not to Buy a Yorkshire Terrier

Newspaper ads listing a variety of different breeds are usually placed by shady outfits that mass-breed dogs in response to the huge demand for popular breeds. In these so-called puppy mills, dogs are produced continually without regard for the physical condition of the breeding bitches. The innocent buyer then pays good money for a puppy that may turn out to be quite different from the norm and may have a low life expectancy. Animals from such breeding outfits are almost always physically unhealthy and emotionally unreliable.

Kennels and pet stores that display dogs in dirty cages should be avoided. Pity may move you to buy such a dog. If you act on this impulse you are indeed rescuing an animal from wretched conditions, but remember that another one will soon suffer in its place. The empty slot you create will not stay empty for long.

Mail-order trade in pets is something I oppose as a matter of principle. These dogs almost always come from mass breeding operations as described above. Even if you receive offers to buy through the mail from a recognized breeder, I urge you, in the dog's interest, to resist! The trauma of being shipped is severe and may leave psychic scars. Any breeder who cooperates with this method of marketing dogs is acting irresponsibly.

Note: The size categories *miniature* and *teacup* are not part of the breed standard! These are classifications used by unscrupulous breeders and dealers since the Yorkshire terrier became so popular. So-called miniatures are usually sold much too early, before they reach a size at which this term is no longer applicable. If you are interested in buying a very small Yorkie, ask your breeder, since some litters include puppies that stay smaller than average, but generally are healthy and develop normally.

Selecting a Puppy

The breeder or dealer probably will present several puppies to you, and making a choice will not be easy. Let your feelings guide you, but also be alert for obvious signs.

Behavior: Is the puppy inquisitive or more reserved? That alone is not sufficient evidence, of course, because breeders who have several dogs keep them in quarters set up especially for them. Consequently, these puppies need a longer "start-up time" when they meet strange people. However, if the puppy repeatedly creeps away and crouches in a corner, trembling or listless, then you should refrain from buying it.

State of health: You can form your own impression of each puppy's individual state of health by being aware of the following:
• A healthy Yorkie puppy is lively, curious, and playful.
• Its eyes are bright, not full of sticky matter or inflamed.
• Its coat is shiny, not tangled and dirty.
• If the dog keeps scratching at its ear, this could be a sign of disease or of inadequate care.
• If the puppy hunches its back when it walks or has a severely bloated belly, these are possible indications of disease. The latter symptom indicates worms.

Vaccinations

Puppies are given their first set of immunizations between seven and twelve weeks of age. They are vaccinated against the dangerous contagious diseases of distemper, infectious canine hepatitis, rabies, leptospirosis, and canine parvovirus (see Vaccination Schedule, page 47). The inoculations are entered in an international vaccination certificate, which the new owner is given when he or she buys the puppy. All future shots your Yorkie receives will be recorded there, too. When you get the certificate, check to make sure it has all the necessary information on it, including both your name and address and those of the breeder. If the certificate is incomplete, you may have problems when you want to enter other countries with your Yorkie.

Worming

Dogs can become infested with worms—roundworms and tapeworms, principally—that harm the intestine and weaken the animals' resistance. Some worms can also be passed on to humans. Consequently, worming the dog on a regular basis is absolutely essential.

The first wormings are done in the second, fourth, sixth, eighth, and twelfth weeks of life, before the puppy leaves the breeder. When you buy a puppy, make sure it has already been wormed. Until the age of one year, young dogs need to be wormed about every two to three months.

For adult dogs, two to three wormings per year usually are sufficient. To avoid stuffing your Yorkie with worming medicines unnecessarily, have the veterinarian examine a fresh stool sample. If necessary, he or she will advise you to worm the puppy and suggest an appropriate medicine.

Feeding Plan

Most breeders give the new owner a feeding plan for the young dog so that it will adjust to a new feeding routine more easily. A sudden change to

The Yorkie has become an indispensable playmate for this child.

different amounts and different kinds of foods often causes stomach and intestinal upsets.

Registration Papers

Every purebred dog that was bred should have pedigree papers. This registration is a document in the legal sense of the word and belongs to the club that has issued it. After the dog's death, the registration has to be returned to the club.

The young family is happy in this soft, cave-like bed.

The American Kennel Club (AKC) registration application must include the name and AKC number of the sire and the dam, information about the puppy's litter, and the name and address of the puppy's new owner. The paperwork usually takes about three to four weeks to process.

Since the litter should have been registered at the time the puppies were born, the breeder or dealer should have the necessary AKC applications at the time of the sale. If the forms are not available, be sure to obtain a signed bill of sale stating the breed, sex, and color of the puppy; the date of birth; and the registered names of the sire and dam, with numbers, if available. This information is vital should you need to contact the AKC in search of your puppy's papers.

If you are buying a puppy from a show-oriented kennel, you may find that the breeder poses some special conditions. In the case of a top-quality animal, the breeder may stipulate terms concerning future mating of the dog. With pet-quality puppies from such kennels, the breeder may agree to sell the dog only if the new owner agrees not to breed it. In the case of a puppy carrying a disqualifying fault, the breeder may even withhold the puppy's registration papers until proof is supplied that the dog has been neutered.

Equipment and Accessories

If at all possible, have all the basic equipment and accessories ready for your new pet before it joins your household. These include:

Dog bed: A good choice is a cave-like bed made of foam and covered with fabric with a deep, thick pile, which will keep your pet warm. These beds are easy to clean in the washing machine, and some come with liners that fit inside. Do not use a wicker basket, as your Yorkie could nibble on the wickerwork and injure itself on broken or split willow shoots; besides, the dog's long hair gets caught on them.

Leash and collar: For the puppy, the special Yorkie show leash, or lead, is adequate. These leashes, made of lightweight, tear-resistant nylon cord, are about 5 to 7 millimeters in diameter. They serve as leash and collar all in one. For older dogs, a leash with an automatic roll-up mechanism is practical.

If you want a leather collar, make sure the inner surface is smooth; otherwise, the hair on the dog's neck easily becomes matted. A cat harness is not suitable for a Yorkie as it limits the dog's mobility too greatly.

Food and water dishes: Use bowls made of earthenware or high-grade steel with a rubber ring on the bottom. They are hard to tip over, do not slide around, and can be washed in boiling water to ensure good hygiene.

Food: Talk to the breeder about the best food to buy for the puppy. Generally, the breeder will give you a small supply of the food the puppy has been accustomed to.

Toys: Best of all are small balls and rings made of solid rubber and toys made of latex. Relatively small chew bones made of rawhide are also highly recommended, since they strengthen the masticatory muscles. You also can give your Yorkie an old sock tied in a knot. Toys made of plastic or materials that splinter easily are not suitable as the Yorkie would quickly chew them to pieces, and might choke.

Grooming tools: At first, all you need to groom the puppy is a comb made of bone, a natural-bristle brush, and an air-cushioned wire brush without nubs.

Pet carrier: One type of carrier is a sturdy plastic or fiberglass box with three closed sides and a little door, usually with metal grating, on the fourth side. Another type is a more flexible carrier bag made of soft fabric, with air holes and at  least one transparent side. Also practical are carrier bags with a built-in collar, so that the dog can put its head outside the bag for air, but cannot jump out through the opening.

Acclimation and Daily Routine

At last the day has arrived: Your puppy is ready to come to its new home. In the first days, you need to spend plenty of time with it, to make adaptation easier and help the puppy get settled. Keep in mind that for the first time in its life the little Yorkie is separated from its mother and littermates, and it is entering a completely unfamiliar environment.

The Trip Home

Pick the puppy up by car, early in the morning, so that plenty of time is left to explore its new home before dark. If you take someone along to drive, you can hold the little dog on your lap to keep it from jumping down or being thrown to the floor if the brakes are applied suddenly. Keep it calm by petting it and talking to it in a soft voice. Be sure to keep paper towels handy, because the puppy might vomit from excitement. If you drive by yourself or take public transportation, use a closable carrier bag with air holes. In a car the puppy should always ride in the back seat. On lengthy car trips, take a break approximately once an hour to let the puppy relieve itself and drink some water.

The First Days at Home

Immediately after arrival, lead the puppy to a place where it can relieve itself. With all the excitement, and after a lengthy ride, that will be a necessity. Put the lightweight nylon leash on the

We all need a break. To keep its beloved shoe from getting lost, this puppy "guards" it even during a nap.

Yorkie to keep it from running away while you are outdoors.

Once you are back at home, allow the puppy enough time to explore, sniff, and observe without being disturbed. The host of new impressions will confuse the young dog at first; consequently, you should avoid having the entire family descend upon the Yorkie and carry it around. Visits from neighbors or acquaintances who want to admire the dog are also best postponed until later.

A place of its own: The very first day, show the puppy its food and water dishes, as well as the place where it will sleep. Let your new little friend help decide what that place is to be. The puppy will not accept just any dark corner—it is too inquisitive to put up with that. Choose a spot that will allow the puppy to watch everything that goes on. Avoid places where the floor is cold or where there are drafts, and do not assign the puppy a spot right next to the radiator. At night, a room temperature of 64.4°F (18°C) is ideal.

A name for the puppy: Give your Yorkie a short, concise name, one that all the members of your family have agreed on. The puppy will quickly learn that it alone is being addressed when it hears the name.

The First Nights

You need to be understanding when your little Yorkie doesn't want to stay alone at night. Until now it has slept

Unless you teach your Yorkie from puppyhood to obey consistently, training it in a relaxed atmosphere and without overdoing things, it may disappoint you later on in daily life or during schooling for the show ring.

With plenty of petting, praise, and consistency, the Yorkie will quickly learn to walk on the leash.

close to the bodies of its siblings, and it is not used to being alone. Put an old, unwashed sweater into the puppy's bed. The familiar smell will comfort it, and it will sense your nearness. Sometimes it also helps to lay a hot-water bottle—wrapped in towels!—in the dog's bed to remind the Yorkie of the body heat of its mother and littermates. The puppy should have free access to its water dish, and near the place where it sleeps there should be a thick layer of newspaper in case it needs to relieve itself.

Don't let incessant whimpering "persuade" you to take the puppy into your own bed. It will never forget these privileges, and from then on it will endeavor to sleep with you. Instead, put the dog's bed next to yours so that you can scratch and pet the Yorkie and give it the feeling that it is not alone.

Picking Up the Puppy

Talk to the puppy before you start to pick it up. Then slide one hand under its chest, using your fingers to hold its front feet together. Put your other hand under its hindquarters. Never lift the puppy by its front legs, head, ears, or neck! That causes it pain and can also lead to injury.

The right way to pick up a puppy: Put one hand under its chest, the other beneath its rear end.

Housebreaking the Puppy

To housebreak your Yorkie as quickly as possible, you have to be very familiar with its behavior. Every puppy develops its own peculiarities, of course, but by close observation you will quickly find out how your dog makes its needs known. You can expect the process of housebreaking the little Yorkie to take about two to four weeks. Though it may be difficult at first, the problem will be solved more easily with plenty of affection, patience, and humor.

How to Recognize the Signs
• The puppy is restless, whimpers or whines, turns in a circle, and sits down repeatedly.
• It sniffs at the floor and, hunched over, looks for a quiet place to relieve itself.
• Some puppies scratch at the door after a short time, or stand in front of the door and demonstrate by whimpering and barking that they need to go out.

If you see these signs, immediately take the puppy either to its designated spot or outside. Praise it once it has been a good dog and done its "business."

Going Out Regularly
Your dog's needs can be controlled to some extent if you take it out after every meal (allowing a little time for the digestive process), every time it wakes up, or just before going to bed. Once the training begins to pay off, praise your Yorkie, pet it, and reward it with small tidbits. Soon it will realize what great achievement was responsible for such benefits.

If you have no yard, you can make do at first, until the puppy is leash trained, with a designated spot in the bathroom. The best material to put down is newspaper, already familiar to your Yorkie from its kennel days. Once your dog is housebroken, it should use this place only in emergencies, such as when it is sick.

Dangers in Your Home and Yard

Source of danger	Possible effects	How to avoid
Balcony	Falling; broken leg; skull fracture	Make balcony safe; safety nets are available in pet stores.
Steep or open stairs	Falling; brain concussion; skull fracture; broken leg	Carry the dog or supervise well; put up child safety gate.
Jumping off table, chair, sofa	Broken leg, at worst, broken neck	Never let the dog sit on a sofa or chair unsupervised when you leave the room. Yorkies like to jump, but can't always judge how dangerous a height is.
Electrical wiring and sockets	Biting through insulation; electric shock	Conceal wiring; leave no live wires exposed; unplug cords when not in use. Watch puppies very carefully. Cover sockets with childproof safety covers (available in electrical appliance stores).
Doors	Getting crushed; getting locked in or out	Look carefully before closing doors.
Broken glass, nails, needles	Injuries in foot area; swallowing foreign bodies	Pick up carefully; don't leave dangerous objects lying around.
Plants	Poisoning; injury	Put poisonous or sharp-spined plants out of dog's reach, or do without them. Vacuum up Christmas tree needles as soon as they drop.
Chemicals, detergents, cleansers	Poisoning; acid burns caused by licking	Keep all chemicals locked up. Don't use chemical weed-killers or pesticides in your garden.

These two have a good understanding. The Yorkie is not afraid of big dogs.

Catching the Puppy in the Act

If you catch the puppy in the act of relieving itself indoors, scold it with a vigorous *"No!"* and take it outdoors at once. Never punish the puppy by hitting it—a raised index finger and a sharp word are enough.

If you don't discover the "little accident" until later, it makes no sense to fuss at the puppy; it would not understand your displeasure. A dog can connect praise and blame only with its present actions. Clean the spot with a disinfectant that is not ecologically harmful, or use a solution of vinegar and water. Dogs tend to keep using the same place if it smells of urine. Pet stores have special products available for this purpose.

The Yorkie's Behavior

The Yorkie, too, has retained behavior patterns and traits of character that are traceable to the progenitor of all dog breeds, the wolf. Every dog understands the international language of its kind, and you, as a dog owner, ought to be familiar with the rudiments of this language as well. That not only makes it easier to train your pet, but also improves your understanding of your dog's behavior.

Body Language

Your Yorkie communicates principally through its body language. It is expressed in the dog's overall posture and in the way it holds its ears and tail. If you observe your dog carefully, you will quickly get to know its own personal way of expressing itself.

Attentiveness: The Yorkie plants its legs firmly on the ground, with its back straight, its ears upright and quivering, and its tail slightly extended. When it is absolutely intent on something, it cocks its head to one side and looks at you with wide-open eyes.

Joy: It is expressed by wagging the tail. On occasion, the Yorkie will also bark at the same time.

Affection: Typically, the Yorkie presses close to your chest and "strokes" your cheeks with its paw.

Uncertainty: If the Yorkie isn't sure how it is supposed to behave in a situation, it repeatedly moves its feet up and down without budging from the spot, and, in between, stands quietly with ears laid back.

Fear and caution: With its back arched and its ears close to its head, the Yorkie disappears into a hiding place. Its curiosity drives it back to the scene of the event after a short while, to see whether the situation has altered in the meantime.

Humility and submissiveness: In a conflict with other dogs, the "underdog" demonstrates its submissiveness by lying down on its back and presenting its unprotected belly and its throat to the victor. If the Yorkie lies down on its back in front of you, it is showing that it feels safe and yields to your authority.

Vocalizations

Dogs have a large repertoire of vocal utterances, which they use to communicate with other members of their species and with the people around them.

Barking: A dog barks to express joy or to issue an invitation to play, but it also barks as a warning, such as when it hears unfamiliar noises. Dogs are not yappers by nature, however—not even Yorkies—they are taught to be that way! That is why, from the very start, you should avoid encouraging your Yorkie by imitating its first attempts to bark. You will only cause it to bark in the future more often and longer than you could wish.

Growling: The Yorkie employs this threatening sound when it meets other dogs that it dislikes or distrusts, or when it hears strange noises that it cannot assign.

Whimpering: This is usually an expression of pain but Yorkies also whimper when they want something to eat or want to go out.

Howling: Yorkies signal their loneliness by howling. This primitive sound is traceable to the wolf's legacy when a wolf separated from its pack would draw attention to itself.

Marking and Sniffing

A male dog marks his territory by urinating in prominent areas such as on tree trunks, posts, and corners of buildings. The next male that passes gets a whiff of this "calling card" and covers his predecessor's scent with his own mark. Only during estrus (see page 53) does a female frequently mark objects with urine, in order to entice males.

Let your Yorkie sniff and mark on walks to its heart's content. This is its way of gathering information about its surroundings and communicating with other dogs.

HOW-TO:
Basic Training

Start training your Yorkie the moment it enters your home. There are times when obeying your commands unhesitatingly can be crucial for the dog, such as in street traffic.

Rules for Training

1. The dog should be trained by only one member of your family.

2. All family members must use the same commands.

3. Consistency and a certain amount of authoritativeness are essential in training. The dog expects clear rules and has to know exactly what it is and is not allowed to do.

1) Learning to walk on the leash is one of the most important lessons.

4. You never train a dog by hitting it; you train it by using a system of rewards, such as praise and treats, and scolding, using a different tone of voice or a threatening voice.

5. Never act affectionate in order to get your dog to come to you so that you can then punish it. That will quickly destroy its trust in you, and thus doom the training to failure.

6. At first, the practice sessions, spread out over the course of the day, should last only a few minutes at most. The puppy will learn the exercises best in the context of play. Show some understanding, however, when the puppy is ready to stop, and respect its daily pattern of activity.

Leash Training
Drawing 1

No puppy is happy when it first feels the constraint of the collar and leash. With a little patience and a few little tricks, however, you can quickly get your pet used to wearing them, despite initial resistance.

• First let the Yorkie wear a light collar for a short time at home, over the space of a few days. Keep the collar loose enough for two of your fingers to fit between it and the dog's neck.

• For the first attempts at walking on leash, it is best to use the special Yorkie show lead (see Equipment and Accessories, page 19). Practice with your dog several times a day, but never for more than 10 to 15 minutes. At first, lead it around in your entrance hall and in the yard; later, use a street that does not have much traffic.

• At first, the little pup will pad along for a few steps, but then it will resist mightily or sit down. Be patient if things don't go well right away, and don't tug too hard on the collar. Keep coaxing the puppy to come to you, and praise it if it comes on its own.

• After every "excursion," take off your Yorkie's collar and leash at home, and praise and pet the puppy. One day it will notice that putting on the leash means that new discoveries and adventures are in the offing. Then defiance will give way to great anticipation when you pick up the leash.

The Come and Sit Commands
Drawing 2

Establish a connection between the exercises and the puppy's feeding. While you prepare its food, have the dog wait in another room. Then call its

2) The sit: Gently push the hindquarters down to the ground.

3) The dog has to learn to let you remove whatever it is holding in its mouth.

name and give the *come* command. Hold the dish, filled with food, at the level of your chest, and order the Yorkie to sit. The dog, as it looks up at you, will automatically sit down. Wait a moment before giving it the food. Once the Yorkie has grasped the command, give edible rewards only occasionally for responding as directed.

If the dog is older, teach it the *sit* this way: Issue the command, then place one hand on the dog's hindquarters and push down gently. If it stays seated—even briefly—praise it.

The No and Out Commands
Drawing 3

These commands are used to teach the dog that some things are not permissible. Respond to undesirable behavior with a stern *"No,"* at the same time holding up the palm of one hand or a threatening index finger.

When your dog has something in its mouth that you want to take from it, gently but firmly hold its muzzle closed while pressing its lips lightly against its teeth. Simultaneously give the *out* command. If the Yorkie lets go of the object, reward it with petting.

The Stay Command
Drawing 4

When it hears the *stay* command, the dog should immediately sit or lie down and remain in its place until you call *come* or come to release it. Obeying this command is very useful and important in many situations, such as when the dog wants to run across a busy street. However, this difficult exercise cannot be learned right away; it takes plenty of patience and perseverance.

First, have the dog sit or lie down and keep the leash slack. While you back away, raise your right palm and say *stay* to signal to the dog that it should not leave its place. Bit by bit, increase the distance between you and your pet. When this part of the exercise is working well, you can then try it without the leash and move even further away from the Yorkie.

Staying Alone

As soon as the Yorkie is familiar with its new surroundings, you can get it used to staying alone for a short while. At first, practice after a lengthy walk, when the young dog is tired.

Leave the room, directing the dog to stay, and try to go outside for 10 to 15 minutes at first. If the Yorkie howls or whimpers in your absence, rush into the room after a few minutes and order it, by forcefully saying *"Out"* or *"Quiet,"* to stop its complaining. If the dog has remained calm, praise it.

Little by little, lengthen the periods of time the dog spends alone. When you reenter the room, call your dog and show it how happy you are to see it again, praising and petting it lavishly.

4) The stay command takes plenty of self-discipline on the dog's part.

The Yorkie enthusiastically makes its approach run,

Contact with Other Members of the Species

It is always hard to predict what course an encounter between two dogs will take. Much depends on the sex of the dogs involved and on the reliability of their character. Healthy dogs kept under proper conditions respond to other dogs in a natural way, and the whole process follows definite rules.

Dogs that are never allowed to have contact with other members of their species cannot learn these rules so give your Yorkie a chance to meet other dogs while it is still a young puppy. Not only will the puppy learn quickly how to behave like a proper dog, but each encounter is also an opportunity to find out just how it fits into the canine social hierarchy. During this phase no harm is likely to come to the puppy from other dogs, for dogs obey an instinctive law that forbids them to bite young animals—assuming the dog in question is not behaviorally disturbed. If you run into a very large dog on a walk you should, for safety's sake, call out to the owner and ask about the animal's behavior. If there is any question, pick up your Yorkie to prevent an encounter.

Nose contact is the first greeting. The dogs sniff noses briefly to find out whether or not they like each other.

The anal check is next. Each dog sniffs the other's rear end. Ethnologists use the term *anal face* to describe the area lying immediately beneath the tail because the anal glands located there impart much of interest to another dog. Male dogs then proceed to lift a leg so that the other dog can smell their marking scent, too. In the course of this ritual it soon becomes clear how much interest the two dogs have in each other and which ranks higher.

clears the hurdle in an elegant leap, and lands safely on the other side.

Out and About with Your Yorkie

Because your Yorkie loves going along wherever you go, it needs to get used to riding in your car as soon as possible. You always have to have the situation under control, however. Prohibit hopping from the front to the back seat from the very outset as sudden braking should place neither you nor your dog in danger. Your dog will be safest in a carrier bag, which you can put on the floor in front of the passenger seat.

The Yorkie's Bad Habits

It is up to you to teach your dog what it is and is not allowed to do; once acquired, bad habits are not so easy to break later on.

Chewing on furniture: Generally your Yorkie will not chew on furniture, but during the teething phase it might enjoy chewing on chair legs, shoes, and rugs. Don't put up with that. Give the puppy a rawhide toy as a substitute.

"Mounting": When a male dog "mounts" someone's leg, it is extremely unpleasant, especially if the person concerned is a stranger. Such behavior should *never* be tolerated. If the dog tries to straddle someone's leg, send it to its bed at once with a sharp *"No."*

Jumping up on people can also be very unpleasant. Your dog might, for example, jump up on strangers when it has dirty paws. You can put a stop to that by training the puppy early, using the *down!* command. Never give it the impression, however, that its friendly greeting is not appreciated. To greet your Yorkie, pet it lavishly, but prohibit jumping up on you right from the start.

HOW-TO:
Spending Time with Your Pet

Keeping Fit with Games and Sports

Every Yorkshire terrier has to be kept busy. The more you ask of your pet, the better. Playing keeps the dog mentally and physically fit, helps release pent-up aggression, and perfectly suits its natural need to be in motion. In addition, it reinforces the bond between owner and pet. Don't overdo things, however. When your Yorkie is tired of playing, respect its wishes and stop.

Issuing an Invitation to Play

Your Yorkie will invite you to play by looking at you expectantly, its front legs flat on the ground and its hindquarters raised up in the air. Its ears pricked, the Yorkie will wag its tail to and fro like a windshield wiper.

Games Yorkies Enjoy

When you encourage your Yorkie to play, you need to schedule enough time to join in the activities. You'll soon notice how much fun you are having as well.

Playing tag is almost always the start of romping around together indoors or out. You run, while your dog chases you. Change direction fairly often, which will train your pet's ability to react as well.

Gentle tussling on the floor indoors or outside in the grass is something your Yorkie will be enthusiastic about. Moreover, it is a welcome substitute for thoroughly normal, playful scuffling with other dogs. During the heat of combat, your pet's euphoria can occasionally change into cockiness and then into aggression. Consequently, you need to keep the dog's high spirits in check and always end the tussling with affectionate scratching and petting. Your dog will then get the message—the game's over!

Playing hide-and-seek is fun for your Yorkie, provided you don't make the game too hard for the dog. While the Yorkie is not watching, hide behind a shrub or a tree outdoors. Then call the dog unexpectedly. It will take up your scent immediately

2) The Yorkie enjoys jumping over low obstacles.

and greet you enthusiastically when it has found you. Shower it with praise when that happens.

While playing this game, you also can practice the *come* command in conjunction with calling your pet's name.

Ball games fascinate all Yorkies. Whether you roll the ball on the ground or throw it, this will be your pet's favorite game. Make sure the ball is the right size, so that the dog can easily carry it in its little mouth.

Throwing a stick requires a little care on your part. Make certain that the ends of the stick are not too sharp; otherwise, your dog could be seriously injured.

Retrieving is something you can teach your pet by throwing a wooden dumbbell (see Drawing 2) and uttering the command *"Bring"* at the same time. You can arrange things so that the dog has to jump or climb over a small obstacle, such as a fallen log, when it retrieves the dumbbell. Praise the Yorkie when it brings the dumbbell to you.

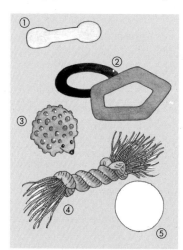

1) Appropriate playthings: wooden dumbbell for retrieving (1), throw rings made of solid rubber (2), latex toy (3), knotted rope (4), solid rubber ball (5).

Concluding a Game

Make sure that you don't lose your authority as "pack leader"; otherwise, your Yorkie will assume that position in the future. When you decide, after a suitable amount of activity, that it's time to quit, terminate the game with the command *"Finish!"* Then your dog will learn that its master or mistress needs a rest too, and that it has to respect the needs of others.

Dog Sports

Most Yorkies are capable of amazing athletic accomplishments and show great enthusiasm for this type of activity. There are a great many kinds of dog sports. Contact dog sport clubs in your area to find out when and where you and your Yorkie can get the right training, possibly under the guidance of an experienced dog handler.

Dog schools: The motto of dog schools is "Learn while you play." You yourself can also take part in the special training programs for small dogs. This type of training is advisable for every dog owner, because it provides

4) After the Yorkie runs through the fabric tunnel, there is a reward waiting.

tips of fundamental importance that can make life with your dog considerably easier. Addresses appear in newsletters of clubs that specialize in such sports.

Agility
Drawings 2, 3, and 4

This form of dog sport, which originated in the United States, is suitable for both dogs and owners. Ask the local organizations of breed clubs for addresses.

Obstacle course: At the dog training ground, the owner and the dog negotiate a course on which obstacles of varying degrees of difficulty are set up. The Yorkie clears hurdles suitable for its size or jumps through a

3) This requires agility: The Yorkie balances its way across a wooden plank.

tire, runs across walkways, or negotiates a series of weave poles in a slalom event. Courage is required to go through the fabric tunnel.

The pet and owner relationship: To appear in competitions, the dog has to obey well, because the obstacles have to be negotiated in a set time and in a set order. Your Yorkie has to react to your signals; it cannot spontaneously take on any obstacle it chooses. The success of the competition depends largely on your pet's trust in you.

Important: Many Yorkies show enormous enthusiasm for this type of activity, but you must make it a rule to never pressure your pet into activities that it doesn't engage in of its own accord, voluntarily.

Grooming a Yorkshire Terrier

For experienced dog owners, grooming means more than just combing its coat. It also includes inspecting and caring for your pet's eyes, ears, teeth, and feet. If performed regularly and consistently, these procedures will do more than make your Yorkie beautiful. Grooming, along with a balanced diet, is the most effective way of preventing disease and parasites.

Basic Grooming Aids

Use only dog care products that are especially designed for the needs of a Yorkshire terrier. Most club newsletters contain ads for mail-order firms or information centers that can advise you (see Useful Literature and Addresses, page 62).

The basic tools include:
• a bone comb (metal will pull out the hair)
• an air-cushioned wire-bristle brush without nubs
• a special moisturizing shampoo
• a rinse that goes with the shampoo
• a mink oil- or jojoba-based grooming spray
• a hair dryer or a small warm-air fan heater
• barrettes and small, coated rubber bands
• a nail file and nail clippers
• scissors with rounded tips
• small clippers or shearer (available in this size only from mail-order firms)
• ear lotion and calcium carbonate (ask your veterinarian)

At last, a nice little stick—but there's no one around to play with. For your puppy's development, it's important that you take time to play with it every day.

Note: For instructions on the Yorkie's coat care, see pages 34–35.

Start Grooming the Puppy Early

Get the puppy used to all the grooming procedures while it is young, in order to avoid having problems later. Since your Yorkie will resist strongly at first, have a second person assist you by keeping a firm hold on the little dog.

Where to groom: From the outset, get the puppy used to standing still on a little pedestal or on the floor, on a nonskid surface, during the entire grooming process.

My tip: Don't use a high table, since your little dog could jump off and incur serious injuries.

Care of the Eyes

Matter that collects in the corners of your Yorkie's eyes, especially after sleep, can be removed carefully with a dampened soft paper tissue. Check daily to see whether grass seeds or a hair may have gotten stuck in your pet's eyes. If so, they have to be removed with a damp cloth, to prevent irritation and inflammation. Then put a few eyedrops (ask your veterinarian) into the eye to soothe it.

Note: Always have eye inflammations treated by the veterinarian. It is important to check your dog's eyes often. Early detection of eye problems, such as cataracts in older dogs, can usually mean a successful medical outcome.

This well-groomed Yorkie's coat glistens in the sun.

You may notice on occasion some mucouslike material forming in the corners of your dog's eyes. This happens to most dogs of all breeds and really isn't something to worry about. Gently wipe the matter out with a soft tissue. Don't confuse this ordinary mucous with an eye discharge, which should receive veterinary attention.

Care of the Ears

Cleaning: If the external part of the ear is very dirty, clean it with a cloth to which ear lotion has been applied.

Leave the cleaning of the sensitive inner ear canals to the veterinarian.

Removing hair inside the ear: Ear wax and dirt cause the hairs inside the ear to stick together, and bacteria to form there. Therefore, you need to pluck hairs growing in the external ear with tweezers about every three months. It is safest to have the veterinarian show you how to remove the hair properly.

Shaving the tips of the ears: About every four to six weeks, shave the upper third of each ear with small clippers (see Basic Grooming Aids, page 32). Trim the

HOW-TO:
Care of the Coat

Grooming a long-haired dog, in this case a Yorkshire terrier, is less time-consuming and difficult than you might think at first. If you can manage to spend about 15 minutes a day taking care of your pet's coat, you will already have fulfilled a major part of the grooming requirements.

Coat Care for Young Yorkies

Grooming the puppy's short coat is not particularly involved or time-consuming. First, give the puppy's hair a good going-over with the wire brush, then comb it smooth. Don't forget the belly and chest hair, because it mats easily if it is not combed daily.

By the age of six to eight months, the Yorkie's hair will be long enough to require more extensive grooming.

1) Part the hair, then brush the coat smooth on both sides of the part.

Combing and Brushing

Unlike other dogs, the Yorkie does not shed twice a year. The few hairs it does lose will come off on the comb and brush.

Preparations: First loosen the hair with the wire brush, to get rid of minor tangles. Then use your fingers to gently separate the remaining knots of hair.

Combing: Always start at the tips of the hair. Hold the hair close to the skin with one hand, and comb through the outermost third until the comb meets no more resistance. Do the same with the remaining two thirds, until the comb glides smoothly along the hair shafts from roots to tips.

Brush massage: After combing, brush the coat thoroughly with the wire brush. Your Yorkie will enjoy this massage. The procedure also removes loose hairs and stimulates circulation. Don't forget to brush the belly and chest hair well, since it tends to mat.

"Finishing the coat": Spray the wire brush with hair spray, and distribute it evenly through the coat with swift strokes of the brush. Next, "polish" the hair with the natural-bristle brush. After you have finished, your Yorkie's coat will have a metallic gleam and hang completely straight.

My tip: After every walk, carefully inspect the dog's coat for souvenirs such as grass pollen or tiny twigs, and remove them at once. That will keep the coat from getting matted.

2) Tying the headfall: With the comb, pull the hair upward and bring it together at the top.

Styling the Hair
Drawings 1 and 2

Making a part: The hair on the Yorkie's body should hang down smoothly on both sides; therefore, even with a young dog you need to use the comb to create a part from the bridge of the nose all the way to the end of the tail (see Drawing 1).

Tying a topknot: The Yorkie's trademark is the tuft of hair held together with a little bow, known as the topknot. It keeps the long hair from hanging in the dog's face and eyes.

• On each side, part the hair from the corner of the eye up toward the ear.
• Gather these sections, along with the hair on the back of the head, into a fall (see Drawing 2).
• Fasten the topknot together in a ponytail with a rubber hair band (.4 inch, or 1 cm, in diameter).
• Over the rubber band, fasten a plastic barrette (with or without a bow).

3) After the Yorkie eats, clean and comb its beard hair.

Caution: Don't pull the hair for the topknot too tight. Never catch part of the skin in the top-knot as that can cause ugly bare patches to develop between the ears, which might be mistaken for baldness or a case of skin fungus. Whenever you work on the head of the dog, watch out not to endanger the eyes.

Other Grooming Procedures
Care of the beard: The Yorkie's beard has to be groomed daily.
• After every meal, use a damp cloth to remove bits of food from your pet's beard and muz-zle area.
• Next, comb the beard and the hair beneath the muzzle. On each side of the dog's head, pull the comb through the hair, start-ing at the bridge of the nose and working downward (see Drawing 3). The long, golden beard—one of the typical Yorkie attributes—can reach all the way to the ground, with proper

grooming. To keep it at that length, however, you have to put it up in curlpapers. Even without being rolled up, though, your Yorkie's beard will reach a considerable length.

Cleaning the hindquarters: Daily coat care also includes checking the Yorkie's rear end, since bits of excrement some-times get caught in the long hair there and form crusts. Remove them with a damp cloth to pre-vent your dog's anal region from becoming badly inflamed.

Setting the Hair in Curlpapers
All the Yorkies that appear in dog shows have long, gorgeous hair. To reach this length, the hair has to be set in curlpapers regularly, after the dog is bathed. This serves only to protect the hair, so that it loses none of its beauty when the dog is romping around in the house and yard.

Setting the hair is also a way of furnishing evidence of the hair texture specified in the breed standard, which is a major crite-rion for judging a show dog.

Hair of poor quality will never reach floor length, no matter how assiduously the owner rolls it; it will reach moderate length, then break off. For additional products needed for setting your dog's hair, as well as setting techniques, see page 58.

Problems with the Coat?
If your Yorkie's hair quickly gets matted again despite all your efforts, it probably has very soft or woolly hair, rather than the silky texture prescribed by the standard, and will then be difficult to groom. Signs of devi-ation from the standard are:
• bulky, black to dark gray hair that may turn brownish later and lacks a silky gleam
• black hair on the head, possibly also mixed with gray-white hair, and far too much hair on the feet

My tip: Arrange for your Yorkie to get a short haircut, with bangs and medium-length hair on the sides of its body. The Yorkshire terrier breed clubs will tell you how to cut your dog's coat properly.

4) Grooming tools: comb (1), natural bristle brush (2), wire brush (3), bow (4), electric hair dryer (5).

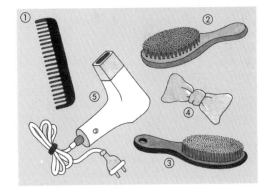

Digging in the sand is fun, but afterwards the dog's coat has to be brushed thoroughly.

remaining hair along the edges of the ears with scissors that have rounded tips. Have an experienced breeder or the veterinarian give you instructions.

Care of the Teeth

While the Yorkie is still a puppy, get it used to regular dental care. Neglect can lead to gingivitis (inflammation of the gums) and tooth loss at an early age.

For prevention: Proper nutrition is a prerequisite for healthy teeth. Let your Yorkie nibble on small rawhide bones fairly frequently. Once a week, rub a soft cloth with some softened calcium carbonate (available in pharmacies) on it over your pet's teeth.

Important: During the teething phase (fifth to seventh month), check the dog's teeth regularly, since some Yorkies' milk teeth don't fall out of their own accord, and have to be pulled by the veterinarian.

Tartar: This takes the form of a hard brownish deposit on the teeth. It is caused by a diet of overly soft foods, and has to be removed by the veterinarian.

Care of the Feet

Once a week, feel the dog's paws and the areas between the footpads, and remove any thorns, splinters, or small rocks that you find. If there is too much hair between the pads, trim it with small scissors.

Overly long nails need to be clipped regularly. The puppy's soft nails can be shortened once a week with a nail file for dogs' nails (available in pet stores). The nails of full-grown dogs have to be trimmed with special clippers about every six to 10 weeks.

At first, have a veterinarian or an experienced breeder show you how to trim the nails correctly, so that you don't unintentionally cut into the part of the nail that contains blood vessels and injure the dog.

Bathing a Yorkie

Unlike us humans, dogs have no sweat glands; instead, they have sebaceous glands that cover the coat with a layer of oil. This "seal" protects the dog against wind and the elements and keeps it from getting literally soaked to the skin when it rains. The natural oils that are washed out of the coat and skin every time the dog is bathed are replenished by the body over time. If you bathe your pet too frequently, however, its body can't produce the substances quickly enough, and its hair and skin often become dry and chapped.

As a rule, it is enough to bathe young dogs between four and eight months old once a month, while adult Yorkies need a bath about every two weeks. Give additional baths as needed.

Getting Ready
Before the bath, use your fingers to loosen all the mats and tangles in the dog's hair, and give its coat a thorough brushing.

Apply a dematting spray (available in pet stores) to stubborn mats, and give it about 10 minutes to take effect. Then use a comb to untangle the hair. If that still doesn't work on heavily knotted areas, cutting them out is the only alternative.

How to Bathe a Yorkie
• Have your Yorkie stand on a nonskid mat in the sink, bathtub, or shower. Be extra careful if you use the sink, however, because the little dog could jump out and be seriously injured.
• Plug your pet's ears with absorbent cotton to keep water out. Rinse its head and body with lukewarm water. To clean its belly, lift the dog's front paws.
• Carefully shampoo the hair on the Yorkie's body, making sure that no foam gets in its eyes.
• Gently massage the shampoo all over the body, including the belly and the rear end, then rinse well.
• To finish, apply a grooming rinse, leaving it on for one or two minutes. Rinse well again.

Alternative to a Bath
Usually you can clean soiled areas with a damp sponge or cloth. If the Yorkie's legs, belly, and paws are dirty after a walk on a rainy day, rinsing off the paws and lower part of the body with plain water is sufficient. The long hair that gets wet when males mark with urine should be wiped off with a damp cloth after every walk as well.

Bathing Prohibited
Puppies and pregnant or nursing females, as well as sick or injured Yorkies, should be bathed only in exceptional cases—and with the utmost care.

Drying Is Important

Never let your dog run around wet as it could catch cold.

- Before blow-drying, blot the Yorkie's wet coat with a towel, but don't rub.
  - Use the lowest setting of the hair dryer, and blow-dry the Yorkie's hair from a distance of about 8 inches (20 cm).
  - Use a wire brush to help dry the dog's hair. Start with the outermost layers of the top coat, working the brush outward toward the tips of the shafts. That will make the hair smoother.
    - To dry the hair on the tail, paws, and head, use a comb instead of the brush.
- When the entire coat is dry and completely combed through, you can "finish" it with a grooming spray that is applied in small amounts to the brush. That will keep the hair from drying out.

My tip: You also can brush your Yorkie dry in front of a small warm-air fan heater at an appropriate distance (at least 12 inches, or 30 cm).

To rinse the Yorkie, lift its front paws so that you can reach its belly as well.

If the Yorkie Has Dandruff

Dandruff in your dog's coat is the result of overly dry skin. That can be caused by frequent bathing, the wrong grooming products, or overly dry air in your home.

Treatment: Use a special dandruff shampoo for dogs (available in pet stores). Follow the manufacturer's directions, and do not finish with the grooming rinse. Generally, the dandruff will disappear after one or two applications.

Important: If what you take to be dandruff does not go away after treatment, consult the veterinarian. There are mites that closely resemble dandruff.

Care in Winter

Feet: To protect the dog's paws from the thawing salt on roads and sidewalks and from splinters of ice in winter, rub petroleum jelly on the footpads before going out for a walk. After the walk, wash the feet in water and apply some hand lotion.

Protection against bad weather: A healthy Yorkie normally has no need to wear a little coat in the winter. In rain or snow, however, it makes sense to have your pet wear one, because it will keep clumps of snow from clinging to its long hair and you will save yourself the trouble of blow-drying the coat afterwards.

My tip: Use only coats made of a smooth material as wool would cause the Yorkie's hair to mat.

Don't let the Yorkie run around wet after its bath. Its coat has to be blow-dried.

Feeding a Yorkshire Terrier

A balanced diet of appropriate foods is the fundamental requirement for keeping your Yorkie healthy and happy well into old age.

Appropriate Foods

Like its ancestor the wolf, the dog is a meat eater, or carnivore. The wolf, however, devours its prey animals down to the very last morsel, including the undigested vegetable matter in their gastrointestinal tract. In this way its organism obtains a supply of protein, as well as the necessary roughage, carbohydrates, vitamins, and minerals such as calcium and phosphorus. The dog needs the same nutrients, which you as its owner have to provide.

Proper nutrition does not mean merely making sure that the diet is well balanced; you also have to provide sufficient variety in your pet's meals at all times.

Commercial Dog Food

Feeding your pet a diet consisting mainly of commercial dog food is very convenient. In addition, you also can rest assured that your Yorkie is getting balanced, healthy meals with all the nutrients, minerals, and vitamins it needs. The composition of commercial food is based on extensive scientific research and is constantly subject to quality controls. Ease of storage is another valuable feature.

Moist food has a water content of 75 percent and is sold in canned form. You can feed your Yorkie a diet of this nutritionally complete food—available in a wide variety of flavors—exclusively. Since eating nothing but canned food causes diarrhea in some dogs, however, it is better to mix it with cereal flakes, rice, vegetables, or dry food (in a ratio of either two parts moist food to one part flakes, or one part moist food to one part flakes).

Semimoist and dry dog foods are far more concentrated and higher in energy than canned food. Semimoist dog food is a compromise between the convenience and palatability of canned food and the cost-effectiveness of dry food. Usually marketed in burger or other "meaty-looking" configurations, semimoist dog food, while more palatable than dry food, sacrifices something in stool firmness and in economy. Moisture ratings are generally around 30 percent for semimoist foods.

These "in-between" foods are useful on trips and at those times when your dog's appetite may be a little sluggish. Semimoist dog food is not widely used by show dog breeders; the majority of its sales are in grocery stores.

To give you a rough idea: 7 ounces (200 g) of dry food has about the same nutritional value as 30 ounces (850 g) of canned food, or 14 ounces (400 g) of meat and 4.4 ounces (125 g) of flakes.

Water: Since both semimoist food and dry food take a lot of water from the dog's body, you have to make sure your Yorkie drinks enough. Always keep its bowl full of fresh tap water, right next to the food dish.

To keep your Yorkie from getting too fat, you have to provide a well-balanced diet. Commercial dog food contains all the important nutrients, vitamins, and minerals that a healthy dog needs.

Important: If your dog is fed dry food exclusively over a lengthy period of time and does not drink enough water, kidney function could be seriously impaired.

My tip: Some commercial products are so hard in texture that a Yorkie could break a tooth on them. In that case, it helps to soften the food with lukewarm water. It will also be easier to digest if mixed with flakes and fresh vegetables.

Home-prepared Meals

If you prepare your Yorkie's meals yourself, you need detailed information about the dog's nutritional requirements. It is not easy to put together a healthy, well-balanced mix of food and at the same time prevent nutritional deficiencies. Also, this daily process is time-consuming.

The essential nutrients—protein, carbohydrates, fats, and minerals—have to be present in the meals you prepare for your pet.

Protein is primarily contained in meat, fish, farmer cheese, and cottage cheese. The diet should consist of roughly 25 to 30 percent protein. Use lean or lightly marbled beef, veal, venison, or horse meat. Ground meat, poultry (always without bones), and organ meats also are well liked by Yorkies. If you use fish, it is best to use boneless fish fillets.

Carbohydrates are found in cereals (oat flakes, wheat flakes), potatoes, rice, corn, and noodles, which you can cook and add to meat. Whole-grain products and flaked products for dogs also make good supplements. If your pet eats predominantly meat, the carbohydrate share of the diet should total 45 percent.

Fats are the chief source of energy for the dog's body. To some extent, they are present in meat. You can also add one teaspoonful of wheat-germ oil

to a home-cooked meal. The dog's meal should contain no more than about 5 percent fat. Young dogs that get a lot of outdoor activity need somewhat more fat than old dogs.

Vitamins, minerals, and trace elements always have to be added to the food. Commercial supplements are available in pet stores. You also can enrich a home-cooked meal with flaked products for dogs that contain all the important vitamins and minerals. Adding bone meal in gelatin or powdered form will improve the dog's bone tissue.

My tip: Add a pinch of salt (but never herbs or spices) to the food every day. Two or three times a week, you might add some cod-liver oil. Chopped vegetables, such as carrots, parsley, onions, or even garlic, provide variety and a supply of other health-promoting trace elements.

Dos and Don'ts for Buying Dog Food

Buy standard-size packages and do not buy large amounts to keep on hand. Once opened, packages should be used as quickly as possible, since the vitamins and minerals in the food deteriorate rapidly and thus lose their effectiveness. Opened cans of food, too, should be kept no more than two days in the refrigerator.

Where to Feed Your Yorkie

Your Yorkie needs a spot where it can enjoy its meals in peace and quiet, undisturbed. Put dishes on a nonskid, easy-to-clean surface such as a place mat.

When and What to Feed Your Yorkie

Get your dog used to eating at set times of day, and stick to that schedule.

All lined up and so still—that's a rare sight. But it's dinner time now!

It is best to feed the Yorkie before its resting phases, but not directly before bedtime, so that it still has enough time to relieve itself.

The number and composition of the meals depend on the dog's age and its needs.

Puppies up to two months old require four meals a day. It is safest to follow the breeder's recommendations during the initial phase and feed the puppy its customary food, to avoid digestive upsets and make it easier for your new housemate to adjust.

At first, about three heaping tablespoons of nutritious food per meal will be sufficient. Once the Yorkie keeps licking its emptied bowl, however, you can feed it more, gradually adding some variety to its diet.

Young dogs, until the teething phase is over at the age of roughly six months, need three meals a day. From then on until their first birthday, when they will be full-grown, they need two to three meals a day, consisting chiefly of meat. During this stage in particular, a healthy, well-balanced diet and the right amounts of food are of great value for the dog's development and growth, as well as the stabilization of its immune system. Nutritional deficiencies in youth are almost impossible to offset later on.

With adult Yorkies it is best to divide the overall food ration into two portions a day.

Old Yorkies no longer need so much protein-rich food; their diet should be higher in carbohydrates, which are easier to digest. The feeding plan, therefore, should contain less meat but more rice and vegetables. Hard, dry food in kibble form should be eliminated from the dog's diet. Pet stores carry special foods for "senior dogs" that contain all the important nutrients for old dogs.

If your Yorkie becomes more disease-prone, work out an appropriate feeding plan with the veterinarian.

How Much to Feed Your Yorkie

Individual Yorkies require different amounts of food, depending on their age, size, temperament, and exercise

Put your puppy on the scale regularly to see whether its weight is in the normal range.

habits. You need to develop a sense for the amount your pet needs.

If the dog doesn't finish its meal, the serving was too large; if it eats voraciously and keeps licking its dish, the portion was too small.

Average Daily Requirement

A fully grown Yorkie needs about 3.5 ounces (100 g) of meat per day with 1 to 1.8 ounces (30-50 g) of flakes.

The Right Weight

Check regularly to make sure your Yorkie is maintaining the correct weight. Simply set your little dog on the scale. The normal weight of an adult Yorkshire terrier is between 4.4 and 6.6 pounds (2–3 kg).

The Figure Test

Try to feel your Yorkie's ribs behind its shoulders at mid-chest level.
• If they are easy to feel, the dog's weight is normal and you can continue to feed it the same amount of food.
• If its ribs, backbone, and hipbones stand out, the dog is too thin. Increase its daily rations, and stimulate its appetite by adding more variety to its diet.
• If you can't feel the dog's ribs, it is too fat. A weight-reducing diet is called for.

Successful Weight Loss

Don't take the Yorkie's excessive weight too lightly, because fat dogs are more susceptible to illness and have a decreased life expectancy.

To help your dog lose weight, reduce its ration to about 60 percent of the usual amount of food, and eliminate sweets from its diet. Also, see that the dog gets more exercise. If necessary, you can consider having your pet fast one day a week.

Feeding Rules

- Always feed your Yorkie in the same place and at the same times.
- Make sure that the dog is able to eat its meals undisturbed.
- Break up relatively large chunks of meat, even if you feed your pet canned dog food. Even a medium-size piece could lodge in its throat (danger of choking).
- The food should be served at room temperature. Never give your pet food straight off the stove or directly from the refrigerator.
- Remove any uneaten food after about 20 minutes, since it spoils quickly. In the summer, leftovers will attract flies and turn sour.
- From the very beginning, get your Yorkie used to eating everything you give it, including fruit, vegetables, and pills. If you give in the first time it turns up its nose and substitute something more to its liking, you will have a fussy gourmet on your hands before you know it.
- Fresh drinking water has to be available at all times.
- Clean the food dish after every meal. Once a day, wash the water bowl well in hot water to prevent buildup of bacteria.

What Not to Feed

- Foods that have been seasoned and leftovers from your table, because the dog's kidneys cannot process herbs and spices. Never feed your dog at the table; you will make your pet into an annoying beggar and harm its health.
- Sweets lead to overweight and promote tartar formation.
- In most dogs, milk causes diarrhea. If this is the case, you should not let your dog have it. Once they are weaned, dogs no longer need milk.
- Make sure there is always fresh water in the bowl at the feeding area.

If the Yorkie is seriously overweight, ask a veterinarian about an appropriate reducing diet. The veterinarian also can sell you special canned diet foods and can check to see whether there may be organic causes at the root of the dog's obesity.

Drinking Water Is Important

The correct drink for your Yorkie is fresh tap water, which should not be too cold and should be changed at least twice a day. Since dogs drink when they need to, rather than "on orders," the water dish has to be accessible for your Yorkie at all times, 24 hours a day.

As mentioned above, milk causes diarrhea in many dogs and is therefore not a suitable drink. Should your Yorkie refuse to drink plain water, you can add some milk to it (in a ratio of one part water to one part milk).

Important: If your Yorkie suddenly starts drinking more than usual, that could be a symptom of illness. See the veterinarian at once.

Treats between Meals

Undoubtedly you will want to spoil your pet from time to time with something special in the form of little treats. Given in moderate amounts, they will not harm your Yorkie but make sure not to overdo it or your Yorkie easily can get too fat.

Before long the other Yorkie will also lay claim to the rawhide shoe.

Buy only treats made especially for dogs (available in all possible variations in pet stores and elsewhere), and never give your pet sweets that you yourself eat.

Bones are not recommended for a Yorkshire terrier, because it literally could lose one or more teeth by gnawing on them. Also, both raw and cooked bones are hard to digest and cause constipation. Poultry bones, too, are unsuitable, since they splinter and can cause internal injuries.

My tip: Always close your garbage can tightly, to keep your curious pet from serving itself from the can.

Dog biscuits and chew bones made of rawhide are far better for gnawing and nibbling. They supplement the Yorkie's daily fare in important ways: Not only is chewing them an enjoyable pastime, but it also prevents tartar formation. After your Yorkie's main meal, allow roughly two hours for the food to digest, then offer the dog a dog biscuit to nibble on. To a certain extent it will function as a "toothbrush" and clean your pet's teeth.

Health Care and Diseases

The prerequisites for keeping your Yorkie in good health are proper nutrition, adequate exercise, and good grooming, along with regular preventive measures such as vaccination and worming and, of course, plenty of affection.

Recognizing Symptoms of Disease

Despite all your care and efforts at prevention, your Yorkie may get sick someday. By then you surely will know your pet so well that you'll immediately notice any change in its behavior.

Indications of Illness
- refusal to eat, for no apparent reason
- apathetic behavior, disinclination to play, increased need for sleep
- temperature higher or lower than normal (see Taking Your Pet's Temperature, page 50)
- dull coat, clouded eyes, dry nose
- constant sneezing, coughing, drooling, or gagging
- frequent scratching or shaking of its head

If you notice any of these signs, consult the veterinarian at once.

Signs of Serious Danger
- There is blood in the dog's stool (possibly in combination with diarrhea) or vomit.
- The Yorkie's gums have turned white.
- When you gently pinch the skin it forms a "tent" that doesn't spring back to normal after you let go.
- Its pupils are extremely narrow or wide.

If you see these signs, take the dog to the veterinarian's office at once.

Hereditary Disease

Yorkies frequently suffer from congenital dislocation of the kneecap, or patellar luxation. Have your dog examined by the veterinarian if it lifts up one of its hind legs or walks on only three legs. Sometimes an operation is necessary, so that your Yorkie can move without pain again after a brief convalescence.

Dangerous Contagious Diseases

Distemper
Signs of illness: High fever, a dry cough, diarrhea, watery discharge from the eyes and nose, vomiting.

Possible sources of infection: Distemper viruses invade the organism through the body's mucous membranes. They are transmitted from dog to dog or introduced on brushes, blankets, and clothing.

Chances of recovery: In young dogs, distemper is almost always fatal; older dogs, if they survive, are left with permanent aftereffect, especially to the nervous system.

Prevention: Regular immunization.

Infectious Canine Hepatitis
Signs of illness: Similar to those of distemper. This disease also occurs in a chronic form that has no visible external symptoms.

Possible sources of infection: This disease is passed on from one dog to

For a puppy, a little stick is a welcome toy. But make sure the ends aren't too sharply pointed.

another through the saliva or the urine. It can also be introduced through contaminated objects.

Chances of recovery: Young dogs are especially threatened. There is usually no cure for them once they are infected. Veterinary medicine is sometimes able to save grown dogs.

Prevention: Regular immunization.

Canine Parvovirus

Parvovirus is hard to diagnose definitely, and it is probably the most insidious of the canine diseases because new strains of the virus keep evolving, strains that are often resistant to the vaccine.

Signs of illness: Serious enteritis (inflammation of the intestinal tract) with frequent vomiting and persistent diarrhea. Apathy, refusal to eat.

Possible sources of infection: This disease spreads from dog to dog by way of their excreta, but it can also be transmitted by the owner through contaminated clothes or shoes. The virus persistently resists many of the common disinfectants.

Chances of recovery: Because of the rapid dehydration caused by this disease, a dog can succumb within a few days. Chance of recovery is better for grown dogs than for puppies.

Prevention: Regular immunization.

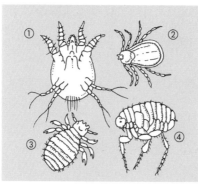

Common external parasites: mite (1), tick (2), louse (3), flea (4).

Rabies

Signs of illness: Abnormal behavior; in some cases salivating, unprovoked biting, swallowing difficulties, convulsions and paralysis, hoarse voice.

Possible sources of infection: The rabies virus is present in the saliva of infected animals and passed on if the saliva enters the bloodstream of another animal through an open wound, such as a bite wound. The virus attacks the nervous system. The saliva of an infected animal is often contagious before there is any sign of illness.

Chances of recovery: None. Full paralysis leads to death. The disease can be fatal to humans as well.

Prevention: Regular immunization.

Important: If you or your dog have had any contact with an animal suspected of being rabid, you have to undergo medical treatment and your dog has to be placed in quarantine for observation. Reporting the disease is mandatory, and health officials have to be notified if there is even a suspicion of rabies.

Common Health Problems

Diarrhea

Signs: The dog's feces are of a soupy or runny consistency.

Possible causes: Wrong diet; eating snow; bacteria, viruses, or worms; a sudden change in diet; nervousness, infection; poisoning (see the veterinarian immediately).

Treatment: If the diarrhea is due to indigestion, give your dog nothing to eat for a day, and instead of water, give it black tea with a pinch of table salt. Starting the next day, give it a small amount of special dog food for upset stomachs (available in pharmacies or pet stores).

Prevention: A healthy diet.

Vaccination Schedule for Preventive Care

Disease	Initial Vaccination	Boosters
Distemper	8 weeks	12 weeks, 16 weeks; annually
Hepatitis	8 weeks	12 weeks; 16 weeks; annually
Canine Parvovirus	8 weeks	12 weeks; 16 weeks; 6 months or annually, depending upon vaccine used.
Rabies	12 weeks	Every 1–3 years, depending upon local and state ordinances.

Important: Vaccinations do not take effect immediately. It takes about one or two weeks for complete immunity to develop.

Constipation
Signs: Little or no stool.

Possible causes: Feeding too much meat or too many bones.

Treatment: You can stimulate evacuation of the dog's bowels with a little butter, evaporated milk, or a few pieces of apple. If the constipation lasts longer than two days, see the veterinarian at once (danger of intestinal obstruction).

Prevention: A healthy diet.

Ear Infections
Signs: Frequent head shaking, tilting the head, scratching the ears, or increased secretion of ear wax. Chronic, untreated ear infections can lead to deafness in dogs.

Possible causes: Ear mites, bacteria, fungi.

Treatment: Have the veterinarian determine the exact cause and carefully follow his or her directions for therapy.

Prevention: Conscientious care of the ears (see page 33).

Internal Parasites

Roundworms
Signs: Bloated belly, hiccuping; in severe cases, lack of appetite, convulsions, apathy.

Possible causes: Dogs get roundworms by picking up the eggs from the feces of other dogs that have worms.

Treatment: Worming. Especially with puppies it is important to adhere to a regular worming schedule (see page 16). After the dog has been wormed, its bed, blankets, and brushes should be disinfected to prevent reinfection.

Prevention: Worming (see page 16).

Tapeworms
Signs: Weight loss; enteritis; muscle cramps; rarely, dragging the rear end along the ground.

Possible causes: Tapeworms cannot be passed on directly from dog to dog; they find their way to the intestines of a new dog by means of an intermediary host (fleas, lice, mice, pork).

Treatment: There are medications against tapeworms, available from veterinarians, that get rid of these parasites very quickly.

Prevention: Worming.

External Parasites

Fleas
Signs: Frequent scratching, especially on the ears and neck.

47

Regular checkups help keep the Yorkie healthy.

Cause: Fleas suck blood, and their bites and crawling around in the fur cause strong itching. Fleas are usually picked up from other dogs.

Treatment: If your dog has fleas, dust it with flea powder, available at pet stores, applying it against the lay of the hair. At the same time, the bed and blankets the dog uses have to be thoroughly dusted or sprayed with an appropriate disinfectant. (If you decide to get a spray, make sure it doesn't contain an ozone-destroying propellant.)

Prevention: There are various kinds of flea collars as well as substances that can be rubbed into the fur to keep fleas off dogs. Ask your veterinarian what he or she recommends. During the summer months especially, you should check your dog for signs of fleas after every walk.

Ticks

Signs: Little specks attached to the skin; often difficult to spot.

Cause: Ticks are encountered with greater frequency in the summer and fall. Attracted by body heat and the fatty acids present in the dog's skin, ticks drop onto the potential host from tall grasses, bushes, or trees, and burrow their mouthparts deep into the skin. They start out small, but after sucking themselves full of blood, they can be the size of a cherry.

Treatment: Remove the parasite as soon as you notice it. Do this by daubing the tick with oil (pet stores sell a special tick oil), thus suffocating it. Then you can pull it out easily by turning it like a screw in a counter-clockwise direction. Pet stores even sell special tick pincers for this purpose. Never simply pull on a tick as you may pull off the body but leave the head embedded in the skin, where it causes infection. If removing ticks bothers you, have the veterinarian do it.

Prevention: Check the skin carefully for ticks when you groom your dog.

Note: In some areas of the United States tick bites can transmit very serious diseases to humans, such as Rocky Mountain spotted fever, Lyme disease, and tularemia. Symptoms include fever, muscle pain, and skin rashes. Consult your physician immediately if you have any of these symptoms.

Mites

Signs: Frequent scratching, especially of the paws, armpits, abdomen, and genital area.

Cause: There are several varieties of mites; all cause severe itching. The parasites are not visible to the naked eye but sometimes can be detected with a magnifying glass as small red or orange dots.

Treatment: Ask your veterinarian or pet dealer for an insecticidal shampoo to wash the affected areas.

Sterilization and Spaying

If you don't want your female dog to go into heat twice a year, you can have her surgically sterilized. This operation, which involves ligation of the Fallopian tubes, is not entirely without its risks, however, and for that reason is not recommended. Spaying—excision of the ovaries—is preferable. Then no sexual cycle can occur. It is best to discuss your pet's particular case with the veterinarian.

The Old Yorkie

A Yorkshire terrier can live up to 15 years and longer, provided it has appropriate living conditions and excellent health care. Many Yorkies remain frisky and cheerful well into old age, while others lose both physical and mental elasticity after a certain age.

At the age of eight to 10, the dog's movements become slower, its loses some of its sharpness of vision and hearing, and it needs more rest. For these reasons, you have to adjust your daily walks to your pet's condition and needs. Also, be understanding if your housebroken Yorkie has occasional lapses about where it relieves itself.

The older the dog gets, the closer is its attachment to its "special" person. Respond with plenty of affection, and don't leave your pet alone too much. Make whatever changes are necessary in its diet. Take an old Yorkie to the veterinarian more frequently for checkups.

The Last Goodbye

If your Yorkie is incurably ill, and if it is in great pain and its life is becoming miserable, then common sense suggests that it is time—after consulting the veterinarian—to release it from its suffering.

Don't leave your friend alone as it begins its final journey! Even if it is difficult for you, you have to be present when your Yorkie is put to sleep. Never let anyone else take your place. When the veterinarian administers the injection, hold your dog in your arms and pet it. You owe that to your companion of many years.

This pet carrier also is a good place to rest.

HOW-TO:
First Aid

Taking Your Pet's Temperature
Drawing 1

A dog's normal body temperature is between 101 and 102°F (38.5-39°C). If it is lower or higher than that, the animal is ill. If your pet's lower abdomen or the inside of its thigh feels unusually warm, yet the dog has not been exerting itself, you need to take its temperature. A warm nose is not a sure sign of fever.

Taking the temperature is easiest if there is someone to help you. One person holds the dog firmly, hands placed under its throat and belly. The second person raises its tail and inserts the thermometer, lubricated with some Vaseline and held level, approximately 1 inch (3 cm) into the rectum. Keep a good grip on the thermometer while the reading is being obtained.

Administering Medicine
Drawings 2, 3, and 4

Tablets, capsules, and pills can be concealed in food, as in ground meat. If the Yorkie spits out the medication, put the tablet directly into its mouth. Open the dog's mouth and lay the pill on the back of its tongue. Then close its little muzzle and hold it shut for a few seconds. The dog will swallow automatically.

Liquid medications should be poured into a disposable plastic syringe (without a needle; available in pharmacies). Lift up the dog's head and pull its lower lip away from the teeth. Then, with the dog's mouth closed, squirt the medicine in small doses between the corner of the mouth and the molars onto the midportion of the tongue (see Drawing 2).

Eyedrops can be trickled inside the lower lid, which you should pull gently downward.

Eye ointment should be placed directly under the upper lid in a "ribbon" about .2 to .4 inch (5-10 mm) in length. Lift the lid slightly to apply the ointment.

Eardrops can be trickled into the dog's ear as you hold its head at an angle. Gently pull the ear upward and rub it gently at the base. That will help the drops disperse.

2) Squirt liquid medications into one side of the dog's mouth.

Poisoning
Symptoms: Vomiting; heavy drooling; sometimes diarrhea; blood in the vomit, stool, or urine; pale or bluish mucous membranes; apathy, convulsions, paralysis, loss of consciousness.

Countermeasures: The dog's chances of survival depend on the nature and amount of the poison ingested, as well as the speed with which countermeasures are taken.

• Take the dog to the veterinarian immediately.

• If the nearest veterinarian is too far away, the Yorkie's stomach has to be emptied as quickly as possible. Using a syringe without a needle, feed the dog a concentrated solution of table salt (1 tablespoon of salt to 3.4 ounces, or 100 ml, water) to induce vomiting (see Drawing 2).

Note: Never give the dog milk, oil, or, worse, castor oil, because with fat-soluble poisons, the symptoms would be aggravated.

• Make sure the Yorkie drinks plenty of water, since water dilutes and, after the vomiting,

1) It is best to have someone help you take the Yorkie's temperature. One person can keep the dog still while the other raises its tail and inserts the thermometer.

will have the same effect as gastric irrigation.

Heat Stroke and Heat Exhaustion
Symptoms: Body temperature as high as 107.6°F (42°C), excessively rapid heartbeat (tachycardia), extreme panting, loss of consciousness, convulsions.

Countermeasures: Take the dog to a cool place at once. If possible, feed it liquid calcium (calcium frubiase is available in ampule form in pharmacies). To stimulate the Yorkie's circulation, trickle five to 10 drops of vinegar onto its tongue. To lower the dangerously high body temperature (109.4°F, or 43°C, and higher is fatal), place cold, wet cloths on the dog's body. Go to the veterinarian immediately.

Insect Stings
A Yorkie that has been stung in the mouth will let out a shrill yowl and shake its head vigorously. To stabilize the dog's circulation, it is best to feed it liquid calcium (calcium frubiase) immediately. Then, if possible, pull out the stinger and cool the area

3) Trickle eyedrops inside the lower lid.

that was stung with cold water or ice cubes. If swelling in the throat area causes difficulty in breathing and swallowing, or if allergic reactions such as vomiting, pumping breathing, and coughing fits result, take the dog to the veterinarian immediately.

Treatment of Injuries
Minor wounds should be cleaned several times a day. Dab the wound dry with a clean gauze cloth, then apply a healing ointment (from the pharmacy).

More serious wounds should always be treated by the veterinarian.
- Cover lightly bleeding wounds with a clean cloth before the trip to the veterinarian.
- If the wounds are bleeding profusely, apply a pressure dressing to stop the bleeding.
- If no pressure dressing is available, apply pressure to the affected area with your fingers to keep the dog from bleeding to death.

Injuries on the feet: To be on the safe side, take the dog to the veterinarian.
- Cover a lightly bleeding wound with a clean handkerchief and wrap gauze bandage or strips of fabric around it.
- If the wound is bleeding profusely, tie off the leg with an elastic bandage above the site of the injury—ideally, above the heel or elbow. Take the dog to the veterinarian without delay. If the trip takes more than half an hour, briefly loosen the bandage every 30 minutes to keep the leg tissue from dying.

Taking the Yorkie to the Veterinarian
The trip to the veterinarian is best made by car. Have someone drive you so you can comfort your dog. In many large cities there are also special pet taxis. Inquire at the local SPCA.

Important: Caution is in order when you are transporting a dog that has been in an accident. Keep the dog immobile and in a reclining position, since you have no idea whether there are internal injuries or broken bones.

It is safest to lay the dog in a plastic tub. You can also make do with a blanket. Have someone help you carry the blanket carefully, with the Yorkie lying on it.

Rules for Visiting the Vet
Dogs don't like these visits, even if they have had no bad experiences. Be prepared for your Yorkie to react with nervousness and fear.

Avoid contact with other animals in the waiting room. If you suspect that your dog may have a contagious disease, wait outside.

4) Trickle eardrops into the ear, then gently massage the base of the ear.

Breeding Yorkshire Terriers

Prerequisites for Breeding

Please don't think that raising Yorkshire terriers is simple. It takes time, money, space, and a lot of knowledge to breed a female Yorkie even once. You also take on a large responsibility by letting your dog have offspring. Especially with small breeds, births are often attended by complications that can lead to the death of the mother or the babies. Many people who want to see their Yorkie have puppies "just once" are unaware of this. By the way, the widespread notion that all female dogs should be given the chance to have puppies at least once is erroneous. People also seldom realize that a single encounter between a bitch in heat and a male dog may result in "breeding."

For those with dreams of making money by raising these popular dogs, let them be warned that such schemes practically never work out. A bitch does not conceive every time she is mated and then produce five or six puppies; two or three per litter is the norm. If, after careful consideration of all the ramifications, you still have your heart set on breeding your bitch, I urge you to join a Yorkshire terrier club, where you have the best opportunity to gather useful information.

Bright eyes and an air of pride tell the story—this Yorkie is at peace with itself and its world.

Time Commitment

Raising puppies requires quite a lot more time than simply keeping a dog. Even the preparations are time-consuming, and you have to be sure that you will be able to pay proper attention to the mother dog and her puppies. Be ready, in particular, to sacrifice sleep. Our bitches inevitably whelp at night, and if, for once, the birth takes place at a more reasonable hour from the human point of view, it is always on a day for which we had made other plans.

Costs

Dogs of breeding quality are considerably more expensive than others. You have to be prepared to pay about twice the normal price for a good bitch. Add to this the routine expenses of keeping a dog plus various items such as the stud fee and the costs involved in finding homes for the puppies.

Accommodations

If you live in a house with a yard and with a small spare room for the whelping box, this is ideal. But choose a room where the noise of the dogs will not disturb neighbors or other people living in the house. The squealing of the young puppies and their first attempts at barking can be rather loud. If you live in a rented apartment, you should get permission from the owner or refrain from raising puppies.

Gather Information

The breeder from whom you bought the puppy is a good source of information. Most breeders are happy to answer questions from their clients. Your Yorkshire terrier club (see Useful Literature and Addresses, page 62) will also furnish information. You meet people there with similar interests with whom you can exchange information and who will give you tips on what to read.

Who's stronger? Behavior patterns are practiced when the dogs play.

Important: If you know from the outset that you will want to exhibit or breed your dog, you should buy a dog that already has its permanent teeth. At eight to 10 months it is also easier to predict the quality and coloration of a Yorkie's coat. Pick a female that is not too small. A somewhat larger animal can deal better with the physical hardships of giving birth.

The Stud

If you are not planning a large-scale breeding program, it is better not to keep your own stud. Instead, have your bitch serviced by another breeder's male dog. Ask other members of your breed club whether they know of a male that might be suitable for your female. His owner will receive a stud fee in an amount agreed upon in advance.

Estrus

A female Yorkie enters estrus—or "comes into heat"—every six to seven months, and it is only then that she is sexually receptive. Estrus, the period of excitement and receptivity, lasts about three weeks. The bitch is more restless and more affectionate than usual. Her vulva swells, and after four or five days a slightly bloody discharge begins. About the tenth day the discharge turns pink, then becomes increasingly paler, and finally colorless. Now she is ready to mate (the veterinarian can also determine the proper time by taking a swab). With "dry heat," the bitch has no vaginal discharge but is nonetheless receptive to the male.

Mating

It is best to take your bitch to the stud on the eleventh and thirteenth days of the estrous cycle. During copulation, the male's penis and corpus cavernosum swell, while the female's vaginal ring constricts—the dogs are "tied" together. The tie can last 15 to 30 minutes. Keep a firm hold on both animals during this time, and wait for them to separate of their own accord. Pulling them apart prematurely and by force could seriously injure the male.

Pregnancy

The gestation period lasts about 60 to 63 days. From the fifth week on,

The whelping box should be roomy and equipped with a little door, to keep the puppies from falling out.

your bitch's little belly will begin to look more rounded. Treat her just as usual, and let her have plenty of exercise outdoors. From now on, however, carry her up and down stairs, and don't let her jump off the sofa.

From the fifth week on feed her a diet that is more nutritious and higher in vitamins, with a higher percentage of meat and vegetables. Add calcium preparations or bone meal to her food. Fresh drinking water has to be available at all times.

Pseudopregnancy

Sometimes a bitch that is not pregnant displays the same behavior as a pregnant dog. Two months after her estrous cycle, her teats become enlarged and produce a little milk. The bitch builds an imaginary nest and looks for a "baby substitute" such as a stuffed toy. Remove the substitute, and try to distract your pet by taking her for frequent walks. Cold vinegar compresses on her teats will reduce the swelling. If her mammary glands become inflamed, see the veterinarian at once.

My tip: A bitch that is experiencing false pregnancy can be employed as a wet nurse for orphaned puppies.

Preparations for the Whelping

The whelping box should be made of wood and measure about 32 × 24 inches (80 × 60 cm), with a height of 12 inches (30 cm). A little door in one side will keep the puppies from falling out. Dowels attached inside the box 2.4 inches (6 cm) above the bottom and 1.6 inches (4 cm) away from the walls will provide the puppies with a space into which they can retreat, to avoid being accidentally crushed by their mother.

Cover the bottom of the box with newspapers and fresh towels, changed regularly. In good time before the whelping date, set the box in a quiet room to let the bitch get used to it.

Care of the bitch: About two weeks before the whelping date, worm your Yorkie. Two days before the date, cut her hair or set it in curlpapers (see page 59). Using clippers, shave her belly with extreme caution, to make her teats easier for the puppies to reach.

Whelping

The surest early indicator that whelping is imminent is the drop in your Yorkie's body temperature to about 98.5°F (37°C). Twelve to 24 hours before that, the bitch often stops eating. Right before giving birth, she pants fairly heavily and excitedly scrapes and scratches a "nest" together. The first contractions have begun. From now on, don't leave her side.

After the Whelping

Make a note of the time of birth and the weight of each puppy. Offer the bitch some refreshment such as a mixture of low-fat farmer cheese, one egg yolk, and dextrose. Afterwards, spoil her with slightly larger portions than usual, as well as nutritious supplements such as farmer cheese, honey, cottage cheese, and a calcium preparation. During the first three weeks watch your bitch for symptoms of restlessness, tremor, or paralysis. They are signs of an attack of eclampsia, which is caused by overexertion and mineral imbalance. Only a calcium injection administered by the veterinarian can save your Yorkie then.

Development of the Puppies

Newborn puppies are covered with dark hair, and their eyes are still closed. Their sense of smell starts to function right away.

Weeks 1 to 3: The puppies lie close to their mother's side, nurse, and spend most of their time sleeping. After about 14 days their eyes open, and a few days later they make their first clumsy efforts to walk.

Weeks 4 to 6: The puppies play a lot and make little journeys of exploration outside the whelping box. Since they now are in the so-called imprinting phase, you should spend plenty of time with them, to help them develop a close relationship with humans.

In the seventh week the socialization phase begins, a time when the puppies practice social behavior, as well as other behavior patterns, as they play with their siblings.

Weeks 11 to 14: This is the ideal time for the puppies to go to new owners, but first, they have to be wormed and vaccinated.

Feeding the Puppies

Until the fourth week, the mother dog feeds her puppies her own breast milk; after that, they need additional food. Mix cooked ground meat or commercial puppy food with soft cereal flakes, fresh vegetables, and calcium and vitamin supplements. For a change you can give them dextrose, egg yolk, honey, and some cottage cheese or certain varieties of baby foods, including beef, veal, or poultry.

Important: The chunks of meat in canned dog food are usually too big for little puppies, so you should break them up. With a potato masher you can reduce the stuff to a good consistency.

Showing Your Yorkshire Terrier

The Purpose of Dog Shows

At shows, dogs are evaluated by judges in terms of their external appearance and their stance and movements on the exhibition bench. The breed standard serves as the basis for the judge's decisions. The avowed purpose of dog shows is to improve the breed and to check the quality of the breeding stock. Although there is much talk of "competition for beauty," the main concern is to keep the breed healthy. When you see all the Yorkshire terriers, their long hair styled to show them off to best advantage, you may have some justifiable doubts. But consider: The purpose of the ribbon is to keep the hair out of the dog's face, and the colorful velvet pedestal serves to better show off this small dog. Walking properly on the leash and general obedience are also taken into account and are skills that one should be able to take for granted in any dog.

Another reason, and not an insignificant one, for showing one's dog at exhibitions is of potential economic importance. Not infrequently, insurance companies turn to exhibition judges or dog clubs to get a monetary estimate of what a dog was worth. In the absence of a show evaluation, insurance companies often reimburse the owner for only part of the cost of replacement; that is, for less than the price of a new puppy. What sentimental value the animal had for its owner is not even taken into consideration.

A pretty picture: The play of the wind in the silky golden hair of this splendidly groomed Yorkie.

Assignment to Classes and Evaluation at Dog Shows

The assignment to a class at a dog show is based on the age of a dog and the titles it has already won:
• The youngest class, the Puppy Class, is for dogs six months to one year old. The Puppy Class is limited to dogs whelped in the United States and Canada.
• The Novice Class (six months or older) is open to dogs that have never won a first prize in any class other than Puppy Class, and have won fewer than three first prizes in the Novice Class itself. The class is limited to dogs whelped in the United States and Canada.
• The Bred by Exhibitor Class is open to all dogs six months of age or older (except champions) exhibited by the breeder (or the breeder's immediate family) as listed in the records of the AKC.
• The American Bred Class is open to dogs six months of age or older (except champions) bred and whelped in the United States.
• The Open Class is open to all dogs six months of age or older. There are no exceptions.

Evaluation Grades

Every dog that enters a show is given an evaluation grade and a brief judge's report:
• The grade "excellent" may be awarded only to a dog that conforms very closely to the breed standard,

A champion—tops in size, type, and color.

demonstrates a calm nature, and displays a flawless posture.
• The grade "very good" describes the same qualities but allows for a few minor flaws.
• The grade "good" is used for dogs that display the traits of their breed but do have defects.
• "Satisfactory" is the term applied to dogs whose appearance doesn't quite match the breed standard or whose physical condition leaves something to be desired.

Getting Ready for the Show

Before you show your Yorkie, attend a dog show as an observer in order to become familiar with the way things are done. As an exhibitor you will have to do the following:
• read the newsletters published by breed clubs to find out the places and times of the shows, as well as the deadlines for entries
• request registration forms from the organizer of each event

- send in the forms, along with the registration fee, to the exhibition management
- take to the show a copy of the pedigree and documentation of any titles awarded, as well as the international vaccination certificate, with evidence of a valid rabies vaccination

Practice Makes Perfect

Presenting the dog in the show ring requires self-discipline and is a matter of practice. Start training your dog early (from about the sixth month on). The Yorkie will have to stand quietly, with its head high and its back straight, on the floor or on a pedestal. It should keep its eyes looking straight ahead. The dog also needs to practice walking smartly and allowing itself to be touched, because the judge will examine its body comprehensively at the show.

My tip: Always think of the show as a type of "sport." It should be an enjoyable activity, never an outlet for exaggerated ambition.

The right way to wrap: Lay a strand on the curlpaper and fold into packets.

Grooming a Show Dog

A show dog needs more elaborate grooming than a regular family pet. Since the judges attach a great deal of importance to the Yorkie's coat, you need to set your pet's hair in curlpapers after every bath. This is done only to protect the hair, not to curl it, since a Yorkie is not supposed to have a curly coat. A Yorkie with its hair rolled up in curlpapers (and possibly protected by a little jacket made of smooth fabric) can continue to run and play in the yard, of course.

Additional grooming supplies for coat care will be needed:
- a wrapping oil, possibly a mink oil-based product
- acid-free papers measuring 7½ × 10 inches (19 × 25 cm) and rubber bands in various sizes
- a special shampoo
- a rinse that gives the hair the nutrients it requires
- a grooming spray for show dogs

These products are available from special mail-order firms (see Useful Literature and Addresses, page 62) or at dog shows.

Setting the Hair

Don't start setting your Yorkie's coat too early. From the eighth month on, you can set the headfall and the hair on the tail; from roughly the fourteenth month you can include the beard hair as well. At first your Yorkie will try to get these "packets" off with its paws. Repeat the procedure until it no longer bothers your pet, and the dog realizes that hair that is "put up" can also have its advantages.

In other respects, groom your young Yorkie's coat in the usual way (see page 34). Brush a little wrapping oil into its coat after every bath and whenever the hair seems very dry. Don't overdo it as too much oil will keep the hair from breathing properly.

At the age of about 15 months, the dog's coat will be long enough to be set all over. The curlpapers have to be placed in at least 14 sites, so that the hair can grow evenly.

• on each side of the body, two to three small packets at the midportion of the outer coat
• one packet on each foreleg and hind leg
• one packet on the chest and possibly one on the chin
• two packets in the beard hair, one on top of the head
• one packet on the tail, to keep the hair from becoming encrusted with feces and urine or from breaking

How to Place the Curlpaper
• Bathe the dog, blow-dry its coat (see page 37), and spray with wrapping oil, then brush again. Finally, use a comb to separate the outer coat into strands of equal width.
• Lay a strand onto a sheet of curlpaper that has been folded lengthwise. Fold the paper around it and hold it firmly in place.
• Then fold the paper up, creating individual sections measuring about 1 inch square (3 × 3 cm). Finally, to hold everything together, slip a rubber band around the packet and make multiple loops.

Caution: Packets that are too close to the dog's body could cause entire clumps of hair to be torn out. Proceed with care.

Redoing packets: Check the wrapped packets of hair every day, and redo any that are loose or dirty or have been chewed on.

Removing the wrappers: On the morning of the show, remove all the curlpapers, then bathe and blow-dry your pet.

Note: An overly long coat gets in the Yorkie's way when it walks, since it keeps stepping on the hair. If the coat is too long, trim it all the way around in an even line, at least .4 inch (1 cm) above the ground.

Grooming the Ears
With small clippers, carefully remove the hair on the upper third of each ear and go over the outer edges again with small scissors. Get the dog used to the clippers slowly. The humming noise may bother it at first.

The packets have to be evenly distributed over the body.

Index

The Yorkie enjoys romping boisterously, even with big dogs.

Useful Literature and Addresses

For Information and Printed Materials

American Society for the Prevention of Cruelty to Animals (ASPCA)
441 East 92nd Street
New York, New York 10028

American Veterinary Medical Association
930 North Meacham Road
Schaumburg, Illinois 60173

Humane Society of the United States
2100 L Street N.W.
Washington, DC 20037

International Kennel Clubs

The American Kennel Club (AKC)
51 Madison Avenue
New York, New York 10038

The Kennel Club
1-4 Clargis Street, Picadilly
London, W7Y 8AB
England

Canadian Kennel Club
2150 Bloor Street
Toronto M6540, Ontario
Canada

Australian National Kennel Council
Royal Show Grounds
Ascot Vale
Victoria
Australia

Irish Kennel Club
41 Harcourt Street
Dublin 2
Ireland

New Zealand Kennel Club
P.O. Box 523
Wellington, 1
New Zealand

The current (1996) Corresponding Secretary for the Yorkshire Terrier Club of America, Inc. is:

Betty Dullinger
R.F.D. 2, Box 104
Kezar Falls, Maine 04047

Since new officers are elected periodically, contact the AKC for the latest information.

Books

In addition to the most recent edition of the official publication of the American Kennel Club, *The Complete Dog Book,* published by Howell Book House, New York, other suggestions include:

Alderton, David. *The Dog Care Manual.* Hauppauge, New York: Barron's Educational Series, 1986.

Baer, Ted. *Communicating with Your Dog.* Hauppauge, New York: Barron's Educational Series, 1989.

——. *How to Teach Your Old Dog New Tricks.* Hauppauge, New York: Barron's Educational Series, 1991.

Frye, Fredric. *First Aid for Your Dog.* Hauppauge, New York: Barron's Educational Series, 1987.

Huxham, Mona. *All About the Yorkshire Terrier.* London, Great Britain: Pelham Books Ltd., 1981.

Kern, Kerry. *The New Terrier Handbook.* Hauppauge, New York: Barron's Educational Series, 1988.

Klever, Ulrich. *The Complete Book of Dog Care.* Hauppauge, New York: Barron's Educational Series, 1989.

Lorenz, Konrad Z. *Man Meets Dog.* London and New York: Penguin Books, 1967.

Pinney, Chris C. *Guide to Home Pet Grooming.* Hauppauge, New York: Barron's Educational Series, 1990.

Smyth, Reginald H. *The Mind of the Dog.* Thomas, London, Great Britain: Bannerstone House, 1961.

Ullmann, Hans-J. *The New Dog Handbook.* Hauppauge, New York: Barron's Educational Series, 1985.

Wrede, Barbara. *Civilizing Your Puppy.* Hauppauge, New York: Barron's Educational Series, 1992.

About the Author

Armin Kriechbaumer has successfully bred small dogs for many years. He edits two periodicals of interest to dog fanciers, *Yorkshire-Terrier-Journal* and *Kleinhundewelt,* and serves as a special judge at dog shows.

About the Photographer

The photos in this book are the work of Sally Anne Thompson, with the exception of those on pages 5 and page 52, which author Armin Kriechbaumer made available.

Early in her career, Sally Anne Thompson decided to specialize in photographing animals. She has a reputation as one of the best photographers of dogs and horses in the world. In addition, she has written a book that provides an introduction to the art and techniques of photographing dogs.

About the Illustrator

György Jankovics, a professionally trained graphic artist, studied at art colleges in Budapest and Hamburg. He draws animal and plant subjects for a number of well-respected publishing houses.

Acknowledgments

The author wishes to thank Yorkie expert Jürgen Grünn for his help with the chapters on breeding and grooming.

The Cover Photos

Front cover: Bloomsbury Masquerade in Love, a 12-month-old bitch and already a Puppy Class Champion.

Back cover: An English champion.

All inquiries should be addressed to:
Barron's Educational Series, Inc.
250 Wireless Boulevard
Hauppauge, NY 11788

International Standard Book No. 0-8120-9750-5

Library of Congress Catalog Card No. 96-21781

Library of Congress Cataloging-in-Publication Data
Kriechbaumer, Armin.
   [*Yorkshire-Terrier.* English]
   Yorkshire terriers : everything about purchase, care, training, diet, diseases, behavior / Armin Kriechbaumer ; consulting editor, Matthew M. Vriends. — 2nd ed.
      p.   cm.
   Includes bibliographical references and index.
   ISBN 0-8120-9750-5
   1. Yorkshire terriers. I. Vriends, Matthew M., 1937–   . II. Title.
SF429.Y6K7513   1996
636.7'6—dc20   96-21781
                                       CIP

Printed in Hong Kong
98

Important Note

This pet owner's manual tells the reader how to buy and care for a Yorkie. The author and the publisher consider it important to point out that the guidelines presented in this book are intended primarily for normally developed young dogs from a good breeder—that is, healthy dogs of excellent character.

Anyone who takes in a fully grown dog should be aware that the animal already has been substantially influenced by human beings. The new owner should watch the dog carefully—including its behavior toward humans—and meet the previous owner. If the dog comes from a shelter, someone there may be able to give you information on the dog's origin and peculiarities.

As a result of bad experiences with humans, some dogs may behave in an unnatural manner or even have a tendency to bite. Such dogs should be taken in only by experienced dog owners. Even well-trained and carefully supervised dogs may damage another person's property or even cause accidents. It is therefore in your own interest to be adequately insured against such eventualities. We strongly urge all dog owners to purchase a liability policy that covers their dog.

Be sure that your dog receives all the necessary vaccinations and wormings; otherwise, the health of humans and animals may be at serious risk. Some canine diseases and parasites are transmissible to humans. If your dog shows symptoms of illness, it is essential to consult a veterinarian. If you think your own health may have been affected, see your doctor.